CONTEMPLATIONS FROM THE HEART

Contemplations from the Heart

Spiritual Reflections on Family, Community, and the Divine

GRACE JI-SUN KIM

RESOURCE *Publications* • Eugene, Oregon

CONTEMPLATIONS FROM THE HEART
Spiritual Reflections on Family, Community, and the Divine

Copyright © 2014 Grace Ji-Sun Kim. All rights reserved. Except for brief quotations in critical publications or reviews, no part of this book may be reproduced in any manner without prior written permission from the publisher. Write: Permissions. Wipf and Stock Publishers, 199 W. 8th Ave., Suite 3, Eugene, OR 97401.

Resource Publications
An Imprint of Wipf and Stock Publishers
199 W. 8th Ave., Suite 3
Eugene, OR 97401

www.wipfandstock.com

ISBN 13: 978-1-62564-542-5

Manufactured in the U.S.A.

Dedicated to my grandmothers

Chin-hal-mun-ni
Wae-hal-mun-ni

Who took care of me during my early childhood in Korea

Contents

Foreword by Dr. Don McKim | ix
Acknowledgments | xiii
Introduction | xvii

Family
1. Does Life Offer Us Second Chances? | 3
2. Life as a Chauffeur | 7
3. Motherhood and Hanging On | 10
4. Balancing Motherhood and Work | 13
5. Redemption and Survival: A Working Mom's Strategy | 17
6. Sharing Stories | 21
7. Immigrant Women and the Church | 24
8. Taking Care of Our Neighbors | 27
9. Remember Soccer Moms and Dot.com Moms | 30

Environmental Concerns
10. Global Climate | 35
11. Taking Care of the Earth | 38
12. Using Less | 42

13 Living Stewards | 45

14 Storms and the Environment | 48

15 Consumption Overload | 51

16 Sustainability | 54

17 Pop Culture and Greed | 57

18 Sustaining Life | 60

Church and Society
19 Overcoming Racism and Building Bridges | 67

20 Peace on Earth and Gun Violence | 75

21 Churches around the World | 78

22 Reimagining Society | 81

23 God and Politics | 85

24 Acting on Injustice | 88

25 Working through Racism | 91

26 Teaching Race in School | 94

27 Immigration | 98

28 Women and Men | 101

29 God, Women and the Church | 104

30 How Can the Church Survive? | 108

Concluding Thoughts | 111

Foreword

The Christian life is complex and each of us journey through it in our own ways. These journeys lead us to different places, to interactions with many people, and to reflect on who we are as individual Christians, as people of faith in churches, and as members of the global family of humanity. All these dimensions are meaningful. All need to be kept in perspective as we move through the zigs and zags we experience throughout our years.

Dr. Grace Ji-Sun Kim has provided an array of contemplations from the heart which speak to us in all facets of our lives. In her honest reflections, we hear the voice of a deeply committed and passionate Christian, a Christian theologian, and a citizen of the world whose care for the world and its people, as well as God's church, is strong.

Dr. Kim's interests are wide-ranging and touch on the deepest realities we know: family, the community, and the Divine. These three aspects of life are always with us, constantly changing, and always calling us toward faithful living, often in complicated situations. Dr. Kim shares concerns that impact her life and addresses them in ways that are candid and authentic. We sense her strong concerns for the things that matter most in life, especially for persons of Christian faith. She addresses world issues, the environment, practices that affect our communities, and the practical challenges of balancing life in the family, as a parent, and as a professional person. We see here a life fully-lived, engaged, and one who is concerned to reach out to understand and enact the desires

Foreword

God has for all persons inside and outside church communities. She lives her vocation in her family setting.

It is important to listen to Dr. Kim's contemplations. She opens doors of understanding, emerging from her cultural contexts and experiences. She has reflected on what she has known and sees in society, calling people of faith to recognize what is happening and to be involved with the problems, opportunities, and challenges Christian people encounter today. Her reflections are a clear call for engagement which goes beyond simple awareness. They move us toward trying to make a difference in our own contexts and the wider world community. It can be easy to become insular, detached, and self-absorbed. But reading this book will startle us and stir us from complacency. We gain new eyes and ears to the world and the church, inviting us to take more active roles in service to the divine calling which summons us to love the world, even as God has done in Jesus Christ (John 3:16).

It is clear that Dr. Kim speaks as a committed Christian and a person deeply rooted in the Christian church. But her personal reflections will also touch and challenge those who may not be part of Christian communities or who have dropped away from church bodies of which they were once a part. It is a distinctive mark of these reflections that they can find their way into the consciousness of those who are not directly associated the church. This is due to the integrity with which Dr. Kim writes in addressing the human condition, human society, and our contemporary culture on topics that touch us all in the important places of our lives: family, community, and the divine. Our families, environment, and church and society are the contexts where our lives take place. The insights Dr. Kim conveys enter our lives and experiences—whoever we are and wherever we find ourselves. Reading her contemplations will spark our own. This book can speak to the hearts of all readers, in one way or another.

The book should also be shared with others. The questions for reflection that conclude each segment provide important and meaningful directions for conversations. These can be held among groups of people, in church settings and beyond. One can envision groups in small clusters of different types engaging Dr. Kim's thoughts, reflecting on them, and sharing their insights with each other. The results can be transformative. "Deep calls to deep" (Psalm 42:7), said the Psalmist. When the deep places of our lives are considered in light of the divine dimensions of reality, new lives can emerge. For personal and group use, this book provides opportunities, as Dr. Kim says, "to slow down and take the time to consider how God works in our lives each day."

God works in and through our lives and experiences. These reflections can open us to see the divine work. We can experience perspectives that can shape new visions for us, the church, our society, and the whole world—all of which God loves.

Donald K. McKim

Acknowledgments

All things happen in community. Communities nurture us, challenge us, and strengthen us. The difficulties we may face, whether they involve families and loved ones or nature and society can be more easily addressed with the help of communities. Different communities have formed me and influenced my theological thinking. Communities have nudged me, provoked me, and sustained me through my various walks of life. It is through community that I wrote this book.

Parts of this book were written during difficult times and other parts when I was experiencing beautiful things in my life. Life's difficulties can either destroy us or help us become bolder and more faithful in our journey with God. They can also reveal opportunities for speaking out and sounding alarms. During much of my difficult times, it was my close family and friends on whom I could lean to help pull me through.

I would like to thank the circle of fellow theological thinkers who walked with me and nurtured me along the way: Fr. Joseph Cheah, the Rev. Jesse Jackson, Drs. Peter Phan, Mary Ann Beavis, Kah-Jin Jeffrey Kuan, Akintunde Akinade, Miguel de La Torre, and Edwin Aponte. I am thankful for their partnership, friendship and for them being part of my walk with God.

I appreciate my friends Mark Koenig, Kee Won Huh, David Hershey, and Katie Mulligan who read the manuscript and offered helpful and insightful suggestions that have made their way into this book. I am moreover deeply grateful to my kind-hearted

Acknowledgments

research assistant, Bruce Marold who has graciously been faithful in his diligent work to prepare this book for submission. His insightful critique, comments, and questions helped strengthen and polish this book.

I am sincerely indebted to Dr. Don McKim for his friendship, encouragement, and kindness. I am thankful for his wonderful Foreword that brings into perspective the important thoughts that I wrestle with daily. His contribution to the theological world and his warmth in nurturing younger scholars' work have both sustained and encouraged me. I am grateful for his depth and insight in bringing theology to the members of our church. He has taught me much.

I thank Christian Amondson, the Assistant Managing Editor at Wipf and Stock, for his assistance from the beginning stages to the final production of this book. I am also thankful to Laura Poncy, the Editorial administrator at Wipf & Stock, for being so patient and understanding with me. Some of the content in this book first appeared on *EthicsDaily.com*, *The Wabash Center Blog*, *The Feminist Wire*, *Feminism In Religion Forum*, *99 Brattle*, and *Bruce Reyes-Chow*'s blog site. They have all graciously given me permission to reuse some of the material for my book.

I must also mention my sister Karen and brother-in-law Bruce for their continuous support in my vocation and my nephew Matthew and niece Naomi for their consistent interest and being delightful conversation partners. I want to thank my father and remember my mother who passed away from lung cancer. My mother prayed for me without ceasing and taught me the importance of constantly reflecting and thinking about God. Much of my mother's spirit is found in the writings found in these pages.

Lastly, I am most thankful to my husband Perry and my three admirable children, Theodore, Elisabeth, and Joshua. My family is incredible in showing their love and support for me. They delight in my small accomplishments and are stunned as I forever wrote more drafts and drafts of this book. My three children are incredible supporters of my work and are a constant source of joy, love and laughter for me. They are talented in more ways that I can ever imagine and were also the subjects of much of my theological reflection in this book. My children's constant love and support for me provides the courage needed to write and finish this work. Their kindness, laughter and insight, provide deep nourishment for my soul. As I watch them grow in their faith, I am encouraged by the hope and love they find in God. God gives each of us precious gifts and my children are those precious gifts from God to me. For the community that is my family, I am profoundly and truly grateful.

Introduction

We live tremendously busy lives. Our non-stop flurry of daily activities becomes complicated as we plug into the world in two or more ways at the same time: by our ever-present telephone, e-mail, text messages, or Facebook. Everything we want is at our fingertips. If we have a smart phone, that statement is probably truer than ever before. In many ways, this is wonderful. We can instantly learn the temperature in India or find out how our stocks are doing. We can catch the news 24 hours a day through our personal computers. We can also stay connected with friends and family all over the world through these four media. And our interconnectedness grows when we add Google+, Twitter, and LinkedIn to Facebook. We have become a society where we are 'plugged-in' at all times.

We have become so reliant on technology that we often become anxious when we are unable to check our email for more than a day or we cannot make a phone call for more than 4 hours. We may experience such moments due to server failures or natural events such as a bad storm. The upside is that we get far better predictions of adverse weather events than ever before. So, we can be good scouts and be prepared. But genuine connectedness, heart to heart, becomes harder, and we have lost the feeling of being connected to God.

With so many stimuli around us, we forget to take the time to "unplug" ourselves and listen to God and watch for God's ways. In our plugged-in culture, people become so self-absorbed that when

Introduction

we go to many public places, we see people listening to music or podcasts on their earphones or scanning electronic devices to check updates that seem so important they cannot wait. We are often among those people.

A long journey down this path can erode our souls. Being constantly bombarded with news and messages distracts us from the need to nurture our spiritual being.

Our busy lives, compounded by the instant access of technology, can result in a life that feels barren and disconnected from our family, our neighbors, and God. When that happens, we must distance ourselves from our everyday technology and try to focus on our calling, the purpose for our creation. We must run less and reflect more in order to nourish our souls so that our life overflows rather than dries out from overuse.

This short book of contemplations and theological meditations encourages us to slow down and take the time to consider how God works in our lives each day. Reflection questions follow each meditation and invite us to explore more fully the ideas presented. The book is designed to be used as a personal devotion or for small group or Bible study groups. It is divided into three categories: family, environment, and church and society. These three major areas are important in our everyday living.

I hope this book will bring joy, spiritual growth and love to your life. May God's mercy, joy and love fill your life, overflowing with it love.

Family

1

Does Life Offer Us Second Chances?[1]

It was the second week of January, and I was alone with our three children. My husband was off to a Mathematics conference in sunny California to present an academic paper. The first night he was away, my youngest son had a little fight with his older sister. He was so upset that he came to me and asked if he could sleep in my room. I automatically said "No," as I have never allowed my children to sleep in my room and wasn't going to start now.

But he put on the saddest, longest face and eventually I caved in and allowed him to sleep in my room.

I didn't sleep a wink that night. And I remembered why I never allow my children to sleep in my room. I am a very light sleeper and any movement or sound will wake me up. My son started off the night by kicking me hard, then like a sleepwalker, he got up and started mumbling in his sleep. He started scratching his arms, which eventually turned into tossing and turning. He woke me up every 30 minutes.

By 4:30 a.m. I was a mess. I told him to get up and go sleep in his own room.

---

1. A version of this reflection first appeared on the Wabash Center Blog Site. http://wabashcenter.typepad.com/coulda_woulda_shoulda/

He promptly left, and I slept peacefully for about two hours until my alarm clock went off at 6:10 a.m.

When he got up, I looked at my youngest son and sternly declared, "You will never sleep with Mommy again!"

He had a surprised look on his face and sheepishly said, "But, what about second chances?"

I said that I don't give second chances, especially when it keeps me up at night. He complained, "You have to give second chances."

That moment he reminded me about 'second chances' was an epiphany. Isn't life about getting second chances? Many people go through life on a terrible path and, thankfully, they are given numerous second chances.

Where would I be without second chances? Where would most of us be without second chances in life? If we are honest with ourselves, we are only where we are because we had second chances. When we think about our faith journey, isn't that a second chance at life? Isn't that the essence of God's grace?

I have now been teaching full-time for eight years, and during those years, I have been given second chances. As I reflect on my early teaching years, there were a lot of "would haves, could haves, and should haves." One of the many "should haves" I experienced was to take better physical care of myself. Yes, that is right, ME!

I had two babies while I was doing my Ph.D. and then had my third child after I finished my doctoral program. I started teaching in 2004 and it felt like I was bulldozing through life.

I wasn't sleeping well, eating well, taking breaks or caring for myself at all. I wasn't exercising regularly. I started to gain weight and have terrible body ailments. Three little children at home was more than I could handle. All three children needed my attention and taking care of them was a full time job. Juggling my children with my teaching position was overwhelming. I was literally racing to feed my children and drive them around town as well as trying to teach, attend faculty meetings, guide students, and write coherent papers. I was overwhelmed with my teaching responsibilities as well as my family obligations.

Does Life Offer Us Second Chances?

It felt like I was driving a car out of control that was heading for a wreck. I was giving myself to family, students and everyone else...everyone except me.

The constant giving came crashing down in the winter of 2008 when my body started to deteriorate. In just two months, I had the flu, an eczema breakout, eye infections, skin rashes, and joint aches. I was even diagnosed with high blood pressure. Something needed to change or I was just going to lose all control and crash.

As women and as mothers, our bodies take a beating. We give birth and do not take the time to allow our bodies to heal. Our body is the last thing we prioritize on our long to-do lists. Thus many of us just collapse at the end of the day.

This was a big "should have." I should have taken better care of myself before my body started to break down.

Now, I work out daily, and I have been for the past three years. I eat a lot of fresh fruit and take my vitamins ritually. I try to make time for myself and to be more conscious about self-care.

Life is about second chances. And yes, I did end up giving my son a second chance the next day, and fortunately, it all worked out well!

We all need to extend to ourselves this grace of second chances, and even third, and fourth chances – as a way to practice offering that privilege to others, like our loved ones. In the midst of all the craziness, deadlines, and expectations of life, we all need to take better care of ourselves- body, mind and soul. We all need second chances: thankfully they are there for us.

Reflection Questions:

1) When have you been offered a second chance? What did you do? What did you learn?
2) When have you been able to give second chances to others? What did you do? What did you learn?

3) "For by the grace are you saved faith through faith....it is the gift of God" (Ephesians 2:8). Perhaps we could see grace as God's "second chance" for us. How have you experienced God's grace? How does this shape your faith?

4) How can you channel God's grace to others?

2

Life as a Chauffeur

As a working mom, September always seem to come like a lion.

Three children mean three school shopping trips. Each child requires new clothes, uniforms, and school supplies. School shopping has become a chore I like less each year.

Getting children to their activities brings more challenges. My elder son has now begun high school, my daughter is in middle school, and my younger son is still in elementary school. Three children in three different schools mean a lot of work for my husband and me. Each child has different interests and each has 4 or 5 extra-curricular activities that take place after school. This adds up to about 3 or 4 different activities each day of the week.

Contrary to how this may make me sound, I am no "tiger mom."

I am a mom who wants to keep my kids busy so that I can *actually* get some work done in the evenings. I have enrolled them in various activities since each one was about 3 or 4 years old. It was all a plan to keep them busy and out of trouble. Since then my kids have grown accustomed to me signing them up for activities. When my youngest grew tired of going to school in the second grade, he yelled, "Mom, why did you have to sign me up for school?"

Enrolling my kids in activities has continued, but now that they are older and more involved with school activities and homework, the strategy of "keeping my kids busy" has backfired. If they didn't have all these activities, I could actually relax and enjoy my evenings and weekends in the peace and comfort of my home. But since I have enrolled them in various music lessons, sports, and school activities, my evenings are shot. I "see" my husband through text messages, and I come home late with more stress than anyone would care to have.

Driving my children to several activities each night of the week and on weekends, even with the help of my husband is exhausting. And this is only September.

I feel overwhelmed as I anticipate nine more months—months punctuated by heavier clothes, icier roads, and blustery cold—with no break in our taxi service to adolescent rehearsals and "first nights."

I know I am not alone in this predicament. Moms and dads all over the nation whether they work outside the home or not, face similar situations—some without the help of a partner. So I send a salute to all my comrade moms who work, raise families, serve as a chauffeur, care for a home, and more—all the while trying to remain sane.

Every night before I go to bed, I ask myself, "What have I got myself into?"

Oh well, tomorrow is another day.

Reflection Questions:

1) We are all in different life stages. Maybe you are a parent, spouse or single. Maybe you are retired and looking back at life or a teenage just starting out. What unique challenges do you have in your life stage?
2) As you navigate this stage of life, what are your survival strategies?

3) How can you encourage other people who are in the same stage of life as you? How can you encourage people who are in a stage of life you once were in: maybe a grandparent encouraging a new parent or a twenty-something encouraging a teenager?

4) What can we do daily to keep sanity and wholeness in our busy lives?

3

Motherhood and Hanging On

A FEW SUMMERS AGO, I dropped off my oldest child at the Johns Hopkins University Center for Talented Youth Summer Program at Dickinson College in Carlisle, Pennsylvania for a three-week program. This was his fourth year in the program, but the first time he enrolled as a residential student.

In so many ways, I had been waiting for this moment. I had been waiting for this moment to come for the 13 years of raising my children: the moment of dropping off my child somewhere so that I would not have to worry about feeding, clothing, or disciplining them. I had been dreaming of dropping off a child so that I would be free for at least 3 weeks. One child less would be a lot easier than having all three children at home.

I had been waiting for this moment to come, so that I would now have more time to "finish" my commentary on *Ezra, Nehemiah, 1 & 2 Chronicles* (WJK). In my mind, I had also looked forward to savoring the moment when I would be less worried about my child who is again "wasting" his time in the summer watching movies and gabbing on Facebook.

In so many ways, I had been waiting for this moment to come, but when it did, it was not what I had imagined it to be. A week passed and I had not made any more progress on my book.

Motherhood and Hanging On

A week passed and I was anxious about my son eating right, sleeping right, and doing what is right. A week passed and I worried that he is using Facebook when he should be studying or sleeping.

A week passed and I found my other two children giving me more stress in an effort to compensate for my oldest son's lack of "stress contribution" to my life.

A week passed and I missed him more than I had expected. I knew that he was busy with classes all day, and extra-curricular activities until bedtime, and I found myself wondering if he still remembered his mom.

The mom who 13 years ago had to juggle studies, nursing, diaper changes, teaching and research to have a family and a career. The mom who wondered numerous times whether she should be raising children and staying at home, or not having children and working. The mom who often had so much self-doubt about doing either well or even doing both at all. The mom who often wanted to escape from the daily challenges or academic expectations and motherhood demands so that the pressure to just "be" will be gone. Did he remember his mom?

That first week, I wondered, and I survived.

Life is challenging for many mothers today as the expectations for us have changed. As we struggle to redefine womanhood and motherhood, let us accept these wonderful changes and modifications. As we live in conflicting situations and colliding worlds, we need to embrace the changes that come our way and just go for life.

Just as life is challenging for mothers, so life is challenging for all of us today. Maybe you are in a difficult phase in life or living in a stressful situation. As you work through conflicting situations, learn to embrace the changes.

I missed you, my son.

Reflection Questions:

1) If you are a parent, what are some of the gifts and challenges you face in parenting? If you are not a parent, what challenges

or joys are you facing now in your relationship with your family?

2) If you are a father, what challenges do you face? What gifts do you bring?

3) As you think about fathers, what unique challenges do fathers face? What unique gifts do they bring?

4) We all have people who have impacted our life, maybe a cousin or a grandparent or a neighbor. What unique challenges and gifts do other people in our families bring?

5) What does it mean to balance work and family?

6) Parents, how do we love our children? Children, how do we love our parents?

4

Balancing Motherhood and Work

YANGON, MYANMAR IS A city of contrasts—beauty mixed with pollution, breathtaking pagodas alongside broken-down homes, fancy malls beside street vendors and open markets, and sidewalk restaurants next to air-conditioned western style restaurants. Everything stands in a sharp contrast with its neighbor. My recent visit provided the opportunity to see the contrasts within my own life in new ways. When I accepted the invitation to speak at the Myanmar Institute of Theology in Yangon, my friends and family criticized me. They were uneasy about my decision to travel to a developing country and warned me about the political unrest and danger I might face. They were especially critical of my decision to take my ten-year-old daughter along with me. Why should a mother of three who is already busy with teaching, writing, doing household chores, and mothering spend eleven days away from home in a volatile country? I have often felt torn between being a good mother and being a reputable scholar. For over a decade, I lived with the constant guilt growing from the tension of trying to establish myself as a scholar and trying to be the best mom I can be. I have felt criticized by other mothers because teaching or research took so much of my time away from my children. On the other side, the academy often criticized me for bringing a child to a scholarly event. They said it made me look more maternal than scholarly. Up until a few years ago I traveled to every American Academy of Religion annual meeting since 1996, giving numerous papers and participating in committee meetings with at least one child at my side.

I tried to rationalize that I was not such a terrible mom by remembering how much I was trying to do. I gave birth to two children during my Ph.D. studies. My third child was born while I was searching for a job. I nursed all three children until they were one and I speak in Korean to them as part of sharing as much of my cultural heritage as possible. I drive my children to Korean school, ballet, soccer, basketball, and school events. I even serve home cooked meals as often as I can. Surely that showed that I was not such a terrible mom, but my doubts still lingered.

In Yangon, I gave three lectures and preached two sermons. At my first lecture, my daughter listened for about forty-five minutes before a local woman came to take her shopping. It was a prearranged shopping event, as I thought she might be bored listening to my three-hour lecture. Later my daughter said that once she left the room she kept thinking, "I want to be with my mom. I want to listen to my mom's lecture." She said she was thoroughly enjoyed listening to my lecture. Because I was saying so many important things, she was disappointed that she had to leave. At that moment I realized that my daughter might have her own ideas about my mothering. She thought I was a great and wonderful mom. In my daughter's eyes, I was the greatest mom in the world, who took her out of school to visit Yangon. I was a fascinating mom who people found interesting enough to come out to hear me speak on a day that the seminary was closed for entrance exams. It was in that moment in Myanmar that I—for the first time—felt whole as a mother and as a scholar. To my daughter, I was not a "terrible" mom. That made all the difference. I did not have to live with the internal tension of trying to please either my Asian culture, which expects a good mother to stay home or the competitive world of theological scholarship, which expects me to continuously contribute to theological discourse. I can be who I am. I traveled half way across the world to realize that I can be both mother and scholar. It does not have to be either/or. All my guilt lifted during that precious moment with my daughter. I have my daughter to thank for this affirmation after struggling to please both sides. She showed me how I can be both scholar and mother at the same time. And Myanmar helped me embrace both the beauty and the struggle inherent in each.

Reflection Questions:

1) We raise children in a very different world then our grandparents did. Most people of that generation stayed close to home and surrounded themselves with people of a similar culture and religion. Like them, we have the opportunity to get on a plane and visit another part of the world. But our world is much more connected then theirs was: we can meet people of other religions and ethnicities right down the block or turn on the computer and be connected to people across the globe in an instant. In what ways is raising children in this global world different from previous generations? How is it more challenging? Is it easier in any way? How do we teach our kids to value our faith tradition in a pluralistic world?

2) Most of us were taught that good parents acted in a certain way. For example, for some of us, a good mother cooked and clean and a good father worked outside the home and made money. Whether we parent in similar ways to our parents, or have formed our own ways of navigating life, we want to be good examples to our kids? In an ever-changing world where our kids may look back one day and see us as "old-fashioned," how do we set good examples that they can learn from and take into the world?

3) Everyone seems to expect something from us, from our jobs to our families. How do you experience being torn between conflicting expectations of others? How do you respond?

4) How do children fulfill the commandment to "honor thy parents"?

5) How do we set up good examples for our children to follow?

5

Redemption and Survival: A Working Mom's Strategy

BEING A MOM IS one of the busiest, fullest, and happiest adventures in life. At the same time, it can be the most challenging, craziest, and disappointing role one can have. Some women we see in the news make motherhood seem trivial and easy, such as Marissa Mayer, CEO of Yahoo, who returned to work soon after giving birth to her first baby. Moms like her make us "regular moms" feel like we are doing something wrong when we complain, sweat, toil, and hang on by our fingernails.

I remember giving birth to my firstborn. It was a hot August day and I was in pain for weeks after the delivery. The stitches fell out, my breasts were sore, my body was stretched and ached for so long that I thought I would never recover. I could not believe that other women returned to their routine so soon after birth. I looked at them and wondered, "What is wrong with me?"

Jump ahead 15 years. I am now a working mom of three beloved children. I can't tell you how busy they keep me. I sometimes can't remember when their soccer games are scheduled or when their piano lessons occur during the week. Every week and every day is a challenge for me to survive as I maneuver my work and the obligations of motherhood.

One of my survival strategies is to expend most of my energy on my oldest child and hope (with crossed fingers) that the goodness will rub off or 'trickle down' to the younger siblings. If I instill good study habits in the oldest child, hopefully the two younger ones will pick them up. If the oldest plays the piano effortlessly, then the younger two will play along, too.

In one way or another, this method has kept me afloat for the past 15 years.

There is a downside to this method, however, as I put less money, energy, and time into the younger two children. When it comes to the third child, hardly anything is spent on him. So little energy is focused on the third child that he is barely thought of throughout the day. I tell everyone that he gets away with everything. This may be true since I simply do not notice his faults or failures.

As the three children started school this past August, it dawned me that my two older children are very busy with their extracurricular activities at school (clubs, choir, orchestra, plays, teams, class vice-president) but my youngest has only been part of choir.

Since I suddenly became aware of his lack of participation, I had a one-on-one talk with him to get him involved at school. He eagerly decided to run for vice-president of his class. Each candidate had to give a short speech and he told me that his was the funniest. He said that he ended his speech with "And this message is approved by Joshua Lee" to which the students all roared with laughter.

Well, the election came and went and he didn't win. He didn't seem disappointed, but trying to be a good mom, I kept assuring him that winning wasn't the point and what was important to be more involved.

The next day at school, he said that students can run for treasurer and that he will give it a try. I told him he didn't have to win, but I strongly encouraged him to run and give it a try.

The next day after school, he came home with a huge smile on his face. He said that he is the new treasurer. A beaming mom, I hugged him a thousand times, kissed him all over his face, and did a little dance with him. My joy didn't come from his being elected treasurer, but that he would finally do more than just sing in the school choir.

I was truly proud of him and who he is becoming. It became a redemptive moment for me as a working mom. With all the busyness that comes with work and raising children, little moments like these make it all worthwhile and a means of saving grace. Redemption is an ongoing event that continues to embrace us with God's faithfulness and mercy. Redemption happens to us at the most unexpected moments of our lives. And when it does, it showers us with love, wholeness and goodness.

I know I will never be the "Marissa Mayer" who makes motherhood seem a "un-interruption" to her life and career. This is not normal for most working moms. Motherhood is an interruption and, in many ways, a good one. Many of us cannot do it all, but we can certainly try to do as much as we can using different methods of parenting.

Somehow, my youngest son being elected treasurer assured me that even with the lack of attention to the two younger ones, all my children will be alright. That somehow things will work out beyond our control, plan or lack of plan.

Later that evening, my youngest son crawled into my bed to give me a goodnight hug. He talked a bit about his day at school and then asked, 'By the way mom... what is a treasurer?"

Gotta love him.

Reflection Questions:

1) What does it look like to love the children in our lives, whether this be our own children, our nieces or nephews, or the children at church or playgroup? How do we demonstrate to children that each one is beautiful, valuable and gifted in many ways?

2) If you have multiple children, what is your survival strategy for raising them? Who can you go to for advice or help when you are feeling overwhelmed?

3) What are some ways we can teach our children about their faith tradition as they grow up? How much of this is the responsibility of the parent and how much of the faith community?

4) Like Joshua, we may work for something and not get it. Yet if we keep working, we may find God had something else in store for us. Have you experienced something like this in your life? What did you learn? How did it feel at your lowest point? How did it feel at the highest point?

6

Sharing Stories

I LOVE A GOOD story.

As children, we grow up with stories. We love to tell stories and hear stories. When I was a little girl, I would love to hear stories from adults. It really didn't matter whether they were telling me fiction, nonfiction, tall tales, exaggerated, or honest reporting. I just loved to listen.

As we get older, we lose this sense of wonder in telling and listening to stories. We become "adults" and want things to be factual, purposeful, and useful. The art of storytelling gets pushed to the margins and we lose sight of the value of telling stories. I must confess that I have lost this admiration of telling stories.

This marvel of storytelling was reaffirmed for me at the inaugural meeting of the Society of Race, Ethnicity and Religion (SRER) on April 26–28 at the Lutheran School of Theology at Chicago and McCormick Theological Seminary.

Stacey Floyd-Thomas, Anthony Pinn, and Miguel A. De La Torre had the vision of carving a space for scholars of color to meet, nurture friendships, and share our scholarship. They initiated, planned, and launched this society, and as a result of their years of dreaming and planning, they were able to create a space where communities of color can gather to discuss among themselves topics of race, ethnicity and religion, and advance their scholarship. This society is to be a place where people of color can engage, learn, and be challenged by communities of color other than our own.

The first society meeting had more than 70 attendees—students, professors, scholars, and activists who attended, participated, and spoke. The plenary speakers were James Cone, M. Shawn Copeland, Barbara Mann, Kwok Pui Lan, Fernando F. Segovia, and George E. "Tink" Tinker. Each speaker provided a breath of fresh air as they spoke about their lives, visions, struggles, and scholarship. The plenary speakers were invited to tell their stories.

The speakers acknowledged the white privilege context in which they are situated in their own institutions and the academy. As minority scholars in such a context, they recognized the importance of sharing their stories of enduring racism, and oppression, as well as the stories of the domination and slavery of their ancestors in the hope of working toward restoration, justice, and reconciliation.

As the plenary speakers shared their individual stories, many of the attendees recognized that the stories being told were their own. The pain in each presenter's story was heartbreaking.

Certainly, the level of pain is different for every person, and it is difficult to compare the journey of each person—the dispossession of the Native Americans, the enslavement of African Americans, the domination of the Hispanics, and the subordination of Asian Americans. The scars we bear from these experiences remain raw.

As the participants listened to these stories of struggling in institutions, the academy, and the larger community and society, we each recognized ourselves within their stories. The process of telling and hearing these stories affirmed for us that we are not alone in our struggles.

Academics, especially those in religious fields, live lonely, solitary lives as we teach, research, and write and present papers. In our loneliness, we feel we are the only ones struggling against structures that exacerbate the isolation of minority scholars in an isolating profession.

By listening to these senior scholars, many of us recognized that we are not alone.

Through the telling of their stories, a life-giving process was occurring. These stories of endurance, aspiration, transformation, and empowerment carried power. As we heard their stories, we found redemption in their voices.

In this way, SRER became an open forum to share our struggles, hear our cries of injustice, and reimagine a world where the Spirit can fill us and the world with power to work toward justice and equality.

There is power in storytelling, so perhaps there is a need to go back to telling and sharing our stories. The Bible is full of stories—of God's love for God's people, of heroes and losers, of fall and redemption, and of faithful people. Perhaps as we reread the Bible, we need to share these stories with our communities as living testament of God's love for us, and for creation and for everything and everyone in it.

Reflection Questions:

1) How have you experienced the power of stories? What makes stories memorable for us?
2) What are some stories you remember as a child?
3) Which stories do you retell young children?
4) Something deep inside of us loves stories. Perhaps it is because God is the ultimate storyteller and we are living in the midst of God's incomplete story. How can we begin to shape our stories so they will be a narrative about God's love, justice, and mercy in our world?

7

Immigrant Women and the Church

IN OUR GLOBALIZING WORLD, people constantly move from one place to another. Within the United States, immigrants from all over the world search for a new life. As immigrants come, they find cultural, social, language and religious differences separating themselves from opportunity.

Immigrant women at times experience difficulties as they seek to connect to the wider society due to the limits imposed by cultural and social barriers. What roles can our churches play in embracing and welcoming immigrant women so that they can integrate themselves within society and become powerful voices and leaders within our churches?

Asian American immigrant women face many such challenges and difficulties as they try to integrate into this new country. The church needs to become a place where women are encouraged and helped to fulfill all their spiritual needs for acceptance, self-growth, and self-actualization. The church needs to support them so that they can flourish.

In many contemporary situations this is not the case. Women are still subordinated to second-class citizenship and are not encouraged to take on leadership position or positions of power that will compete with Asian American men.

My experiences of surviving in two cultures, American and Korean, have illustrated these problems and difficulties.

When I started seminary as a young woman at the age of 23, Korean male pastors and students told me that studying was not as important as getting married. Then after I did get married and started my Ph.D. program, the male Korean pastors and students all told me that having a child was more important than starting my doctoral program. And when during my comprehensive exams, I gave birth to my first child, Korean and Korean American male pastors said that I should drop out of school, have another child and "be their mom."

There was no encouragement or solidarity from the Korean and Korean American male students or pastors. All they wanted to do was impose their male patriarchal understanding of the roles of the woman onto me.

This ordeal with Korean and Korean American men was extremely painful and unforgettable. It laid great burdens on my life as I struggled to study as well as survive in a bi-cultural patriarchal society that deems women worthless unless they were married mothers with children.

This is my story. Other women's stories also tell of dealing with such criticisms and stereotypes. It is something we must recognize. It is something we need to fight. It is something that needs to be overcome.

If the church is to survive, it must become stronger by fulfilling and using all its members. It cannot leave half of its members behind. It needs to forget separation, forget "co-anything," and celebrate all its members so that everyone thrives, flourishes and embraces their full humanity.

Reflection Questions:

1) We all have a story that is filled with ups and downs, triumphs and heartaches. What challenges have you faced in your life? Who has told you that you would never make it? How did you respond?

Contemplations from the Heart

2) How do you embrace the life of immigrants into your own daily life?

3) In this global world, what steps can we take to welcome, and embrace those from whom we differ?

8

Taking Care of Our Neighbors

MOST PEOPLE PROBABLY GET tired of hearing about politics as the election cycle returns every four years. The campaign always seems too long. As soon as one election ends and goes it seems the next election cycle starts.

As elections occur, people ask the recurring question of whether this election is about either "social issues" or the "economy"? However, is there a real difference between the two? Are social issues that much different or set apart from economic issues of our time?

The social issues that the political analysts, media, and the voters raise include issues of women's health, gay marriages, contraceptives, abortion, equal rights, and equal pay for women, and equitable health care. These issues appear to divide the voters into two very different camps. As voters and analysts argue that the key factor or issue is the economy, we need to ask ourselves, "How are these social issues separate from economic issues?"

Every time someone has to pay out of their pocket for contraceptives or any other health matter, it affects their personal household economics. It may mean a decrease in other spending because they spend more for health care. When a woman makes a decision whether to bear a child or to abort the child, it has huge economic consequences for her, her family, and society.

When gays and lesbians who are in committed relationships want to get married, it has huge implications on their income taxes, spousal benefits, and inheritance taxes. How can gay marriage not be an economic issue?

When a woman seeks equal pay for equal work, how can this not be an economic issue? Americans need to recognize that social and economic issues are intertwined. Americans need to recognize the importance of these social issues and how they impact our personal and national pocket books.

We need to recognize the implications of who is elected president every four years and how that person's perspectives on so-called social or women's issues will affect individual's economies as well as the national and world-wide economy.

Don't let anyone fool you that social issues and economic issues are two different and distinct concerns within any election. They are one and the same issue. Please vote wisely.

Reflection Questions:

1) Voters like to raise the question of taxes and how much should we be paying and what governments should be doing with them. How can we be good steward of our money and resources?

2) What is your biblical reflection on "Give to Caesar what is Caesar's and to God what belongs to God"? (Mark 12:17)

3) How can we become more intentional voters who are guided by what the gospel teaches us about the poor, the lonely, the imprisoned and the naked? "For I was hungry and you gave me something to eat, I was thirsty and you gave me something to drink, I was a stranger and you invited me in, I needed clothes and you clothed me, I was sick and you looked after me, I was in prison and you came to visit me." (Matthew 25:35).

4) How can we become more involved in the political process so that we can influence laws and policies to help our sisters and brothers who are in the greatest need?

9

Remember Soccer Moms and Dot.com Moms

BEING A MOM THESE days requires lots of skills. It is like being Cinderella in reverse. Moms are laundress, cook, cleaner, chauffeur, and scullery maid all at once for children rather than stepsisters. At times, I feel inadequate.

As a mother of three children (one in high school, one in middle school and one in elementary school), I know how difficult it is to juggle being a mom and having a full-time job: it means being pulled in all directions, with children asking for something for a school project due tomorrow, as well as driving them across town to a soccer or ballet lesson.

I find myself in the midst of this hurricane every night, including weekends. Sometimes, I am amazed that I am able to manage their schedules as well as my own work schedule.

Moms are multitasking everywhere. For me, an hour-long phone conversation also means time to do the dusting and make sure my stove is spic and span. Then I begin with the chauffeuring. Moms know how to get things done, and a term that captures this idea is "soccer mom."

Remember Soccer Moms and Dot.com Moms

The term "soccer mom" came into widespread usage during the 1996 U.S. presidential election. It refers to middle-class suburban working moms who spend a lot of time driving their children around to sports and other extra-curricular activities. The term was used frequently during the elections, as the soccer moms played a key role.

Mothers embraced this endearing term as it expressed their multitasking. Many soccer moms are overburdened and overwhelmed with responsibilities at work and at home. Many feel they need to work extra hard to prove themselves at the office and to prove that they are also good, loving moms at home.

Yes, I, like many others, fall into that category.

Fast-forward to 2012 and another election. Today, we still widely use the term soccer mom, but another term is emerging: the "dot.com mom." Dot.com moms are still the suburban middle-class working moms who continue to drive children around to sports and extracurricular activities. But they are connected to and active in the realm of social media.

Dot.com moms consult each other before buying things online. They use social media to discuss child rearing and they influence some of the day's key social media concerns. While Internet use is rising, it is important to reflect how much influence dot.com moms can have not only on the general election but also on the world.

Dot.com moms at work are connected to social media throughout the day and can have a major influence on what goes on daily in our communities, cities, and nation. For millennia, women have been subjugated in family and society. But with the rise of soccer moms and now dot.com moms, the world will feel the intellectual equality of women translated into political power. That will end ideas that relegate women to the home, typewriter, and rectal thermometer. The influence that dot.com moms can have on advertising, politics, education, and religion has begun, and its horizon is broad and beckoning.

Presidential candidates as well as other candidates for other offices must pay careful attention to the dot.com moms and their concerns. Politicians on all levels need to respond to ideas that address the crucial needs of women, like women's health, equal pay, tax cuts on the middle-class, abortion, unrestricted marriage, and rights over their own bodies. If candidates do not take women's concerns seriously, it may cost them at the polls.

Reflection Questions

1) How has the influx of social media changed your life?
2) How can we better use social media to build women's lives and characters?
3) How can we implement social media in our daily lives for furthering the work of peace, justice and love? It can be done. How will you participate?

Environmental Concerns

10

Global Climate

MAJOR WEATHER PATTERN CHANGES should alarm everyone. Anne Thompson is NBC News' Chief Environmental Affairs correspondent, recently reported that the average temperature in our climate has increased by one degree Celsius (almost two degrees Fahrenheit) over the past century. To someone who is not a scientist, this might not sound too alarming at first, but a one degree change in our average temperature can have devastating effects on our climate and therefore on the environment. A change of the average temperature in the arctic regions from 32° F to 33° F can lead to melting ice caps that raise the levels of oceans by several inches.

With warmer climates, we experience less precipitation. We have drier summers and less snow in the winter which affects the flora on the land on which we live. Droughts last longer and land that once could be farmed can no longer yield any food. Farmlands in Africa are moving south as the Sahara becomes larger and the desert moves south.

We are also seeing species migrate to temperatures where they can survive. This change in migratory habits puts stress on them and stress on the habitats to which they move. Scientists have determined that a crab's heart will stop beating with the increase of only two degrees Fahrenheit. This means that crabs will be at their limit of survivability if temperatures keep rising. Butterflies that used to fly in Texas are now found in the Northeast and the ice in Greenland is melting faster than anyone had earlier imagined.

As our weather warms it affects our livelihood. Much of the change in climate is due to our abuse of the planet and its resources. Through globalization and consumerism, we create new environmental problems such as depletion of the earth's ozone layer, rising temperatures, surprising weather patterns, rainforest destruction, steady depletion of groundwater, proliferation of nuclear wastes, and the pending mass production of genetically altered foodstuffs. These problems illustrate the incompatibility of our present global economic system and a healthy, sustainable environment.

The global economic priorities of the twenty-first century are simply not compatible with the need to prevent its industrial and economic activities from destroying the global ecological balance. *The Report on Alternatives to Economic Globalization* states: "Economic globalization is intrinsically harmful to the environment because it is based on ever-increasing consumption, exploitation of resources, and waste disposal problems." [2]

The climate is our planet's largest, most important, and most vulnerable system. It sustains life. Climate changes have grave consequences. We cannot carry on with our lives as usual and ignore the massive changes our lifestyle causes.

Most of us know firsthand the temptation to exploit the vulnerability of other people, the world's flora and fauna, and the land. We are either the exploiter or the exploited; often we are both. Now we face the consequences of exploiting the defenseless inhabitants of the earth. The earth cries out against the terrible damage that we cause as we are ceaselessly exploiting nature.

There is no time left for further denial or delayed action with regard to global warming. Denial has been stripped away by our changing weather, although large segments of our neighbors, including far too many in our own country have not yet accepted the need for change. Global warming tells us we cannot continue

---

2. Grace Ji-Sun Kim, *The Holy Spirit, Chi, and the Other* (New York: Palgrave Macmillan, 2011), 67.

to live selfishly, heedless of the consequences of our profligate behavior.

The tipping point of a global thermal catastrophe may be less than a few decades away. We are part of the entire biosphere that creates, gives and sustains all life here on earth. Thus, we damage our health by damaging the earth. We cannot live without the earth.

We, and all the other inhabitants on this planet, need the earth in a sustainable, healthy state for survival. Preserving the health and wealth of our planet must be one of our highest priorities. We have no other earth on which to live. We must stop our habits of wasting natural resources and polluting our air, water and land. Without the planet, we cannot exist; therefore, we must begin a new relationship with the environment now and for generations to come.

Reflections Questions:

1) What event in the Bible describes what can be considered a warning against global warming?

2) What does it look like for you, as an individual, to care for God's creation on a daily basis? How can your work as an individual translate into greater work in communities, states, nations and the world?

3) Make a list of two to three actions you will take to better care for God's creation, perhaps things that will even work to restore and save it!

11

Taking Care of the Earth

CONTRARY TO CONVENTIONAL WISDOM, it appears that money has little effect on happiness. Rather, the conspicuous consumption that money allows creates stress on humans and on nature leading to imbalances that amount to injustice. Bloated by consumption; we need to develop a new perspective on our living and our planet rooted in how God calls us to live.

Our environmental habits lead us to destruction. We must recognize the terrible path we are on, so we can find a new way to preserve the wealth of our planet instead of leaving a barren desert for our posterity. Climate change deepens the injustice between rich and poor. The rich can grow richer from exploitation and move their residence to the most desirable climate. They can even create synthetic weather at will through technology. The poor are stuck where they are, where the means of creating wealth disappear. Without the strong participation of local communities and states throughout the world, political systems have little hope of changing practices that harm the environment.

One individual or group alone cannot bring about the needed change in how we live. We must all work toward a goal of planetary protection. Just ways of managing the earth are necessary as we work toward just living. Unjust distribution of resources and goods leads to unhealthy ways of living that include overuse of goods, misuse of natural resources, and pollution all of which knows no borders. Faith communities need to join together to act immediately if eco-justice is to be achieved. Partnership is crucial. For many lands and peoples, the time may already be too late.

The word *oikos* (Greek for "house"), which is the base of the word *ecology*, is also the linguistic root for economics and ecumenicity. There is a connection between our domestic economics and our stewardship of the earth's economics.

As we search for just ways of living together, we need to find common ground on economic policies that can guide us to live sustainably and justly on our earth. Economics, ecology, and theology need to be tied more closely together, rather than separated as we have done thus far.

Indigenous economies teach us that sharing natural resources is a basic requirement for all inhabitants on this earth to flourish. When one group hoards resources, another group will suffer.

Ecology is not and should not be a pastime for birdwatchers or "tree huggers." Rather, it is an urgent discourse that we must all seriously engage in because it is essential to life and all that life encompasses.

Resources need time to replenish but the lifestyle we have adopted does not give enough time for replenishment to occur. Furthermore, energy sources are running out quickly while demands for energy increase. We must understand the large problem we are creating and learn to exchange our greed for stewardship.

Countries that saw early industrialization (North America and Western Europe) consume too many of the world's resources. Countries now developing (South and East Asia, and parts of South America and Africa) are imitating those bad habits.

One concrete mission of the church is to model, endorse, and promote life by revering the earth and its entire people and by turning back the kind of uncritical exploitation, which we adopted in the modern age. Created by God, we are members of the family of God.

As God's family, we need to learn how to cohabit with other creatures and created things to live sustainably. To "sustain" means to live in fellowship, friendship, and caring for others with comfort, protection and sympathy. As we strive for a sustainable life, which seeks the good of all created beings and not just ourselves, we will find ourselves flourishing at a deeper level than before. For all beings to flourish, we must improve on the model of the world's predators, who survive by preying on the weak and the young. In the Peaceable Kin-dom, the lion must change her ways in order to lie down with the lamb.

As we reflect theologically on this problem, and as we find ourselves deeply complicit in the destruction of the environment, we can rethink our understanding of God, creation, and each other, and choose to act justly. By pursuing a deeper level of engagement with biblical sources – an engagement consciously rejecting the interpretive grid of colonial power structures – we can rediscover and begin to live in the power of God's transforming love.

The gospel unequivocally calls us to love God with all our heart, soul, mind and strength, and to love our neighbor as ourselves (Matthew 22:36–38). We cannot claim to love God yet oppress and neglect our neighbor. Both the Hebrew and Christian Scriptures equate pursuing economic justice with knowing and serving God.

Jesus, whom we are called through the power of God's Spirit to imitate, identified completely with marginalized people and placed serving the poorest people of the world at the very heart of knowing God:

> For I was hungry and you gave me something to eat, I was thirsty and you gave me something to drink, I was a stranger and you invited me in, I was naked and you clothed me, I was sick and you looked after me, I was in prison and you came to visit me ... I tell you the truth, whatever you did for one of the least of these ... you did for me (Matthew 25:35, 36, 40).

At their core, selfishness and greed are idolatry, an exaltation of the self that leads to death. God is the Spirit who has breathed life into all of us. As God gives us life, we can come to understand how the Creator is present in us and in all creation.

Our own recognition of God's presence will help us work toward restoration and reconciliation with each other and the earth. It is the Spirit of God who gives abundant life and who can transform our lives so that we can begin to take steps to reverse some of the injustices that we have caused on the earth and toward each other.

Reflection Questions:

1) What makes you most happy? Is it family, friends, money or something else? If you live in pursuit of this happiness, what sort of choices do you make on a regular basis?

2) How are your choices contributing to the destruction of God's ecology (*oikos*)? How are they building it up?

3) In light of this discussion on saving the planet, how can we faithfully love God and our neighbor (Matthew 22:36–38)? What does this entail?

4) What does it mean for creation to be viewed as among "the least of these?"

12

Using Less

RAISING CHILDREN MEANS PACKING school lunches, including a drink. Water, in our privileged context, is always a safe and preferred choice, but our household dilemma is how to send water with them. We often use water bottles, preferably reusable ones, purchased in the supermarket. These bottles, whether reusable or disposable, have become a way of life for many of us today. I see water bottles everywhere.

It is not unusual to be served a bottle of water in friends' homes, schools, churches, and anywhere people gather. Reusable, washable cups have all but disappeared. It appears we can only drink water from a bottle.

We cannot seem to drink simply from a cup using filtered tap water. We have forgotten that water does not come in a bottle, and that we can get water from a water fountain, kitchen sink, or filtration jug. We have fallen into a lifestyle of comfort, ease and convenience, where disposable dining ware is preferable to reusable items.

We think that washing cups is an inconvenience and that bottled water is cleaner and safer than tap water (this may be true, but only in certain places around the world). We think our bright

Using Less

red, disposable cup is cheaper than spending money on the hot water, soap, and special brushes needed to clean some glasses.

Perhaps we just like to throw things out after use. But where do all these water bottles end up? In 2008, Americans drank an average of 215 bottles of water per person. Roughly 50 billion plastic water bottles end up in U.S. landfills every year. That is roughly 140 million every day—enough bottles to reach China and back.

Since many of us never set eyes on a landfill, we fail to see our contributions to it. We live with the mentality of "out of sight, out of mind" and have become so complacent and busy that we rarely stop to think of the damage we are causing planet Earth. Water has become commercialized and we send 1 billion water bottles a week around the U.S. Manufacturing plastic bottles causes pollution in the production process as it uses petrochemical resources. Shipping bottles across the country, along with all other bottled or canned beverages, uses fuel and further pollutes the air with diesel fumes.

The environmental impact is huge. Plastic takes more than 700 years to decompose, and the amount of oil used to produce water bottles yearly could fuel more than 1 million cars for a year. As we continue to use disposable plastic bottles, we are neglecting to be good stewards of the Earth.

We need to get back to the basics and start using glasses that we can wash and reuse with soaps that contain no polluting detergents. We need to understand that filtering tap water is clean and efficient.

We need to teach our children about sustainability and care for creation as our silence and neglect will continue to harm the environment. We must raise children to understand that water did not always come in a bottle. The water bottle is a human invention to make our lifestyles easier, but an invention with a heavy price. Excessive use and disposal of plastic bottles will continue to damage our environment unless diligence is exercised in recycling and in selective use for people with communicable diseases or in hospitals.

We cannot reverse the damage we have inflicted unless we stop our destructive habits.

As water bottles fill our landfills, they become more hazardous waste and they consume useable land, which affects our quality of life today and for future generations.

We need to be mindful of our habits and shift toward faithful stewardship and sustainable ways of living. Our grandparents did fine without plastic bottles. Maybe the assumption that newer is better is not right. Maybe our grandparents were on to something. Not only is carrying a reusable water bottle better for the environment, it is cheaper too. And unless you are reading this in a third world country, your tap water is just as good as bottled water. Try a reusable bottle for yourself, your wallet, and the world.

So, the next time you feel the urge to buy disposable water bottles, pause to think about the pollution and waste it causes the planet Earth, which was created by God and should not be polluted or defiled. Water is a gift from the Earth. It should not be bottled up. It should flow freely so that all may enjoy it in the future. Even more, water is absolutely essential to life. Imagine Earth like Mars, with all the water gone or, more likely, all the water polluted beyond reclamation.

Reflection Questions:

1) What do you pack to eat and drink at work, picnics or getaways? Are they recyclable products or throwaway items?

2) What can you do as an individual to prevent more garbage in our landfills? What might you do in your community, perhaps lead a project, to achieve the same goal?

3) What can you do to reduce your everyday water usage?

4) What would help you reduce, reuse, and recycle water and other resources?

5) How plentiful or scarce is water where you live? Does this change how you perceive and use water?

13

Living Stewards

The Carnival cruise ship "Triumph" made headlines in February 2013 when it lost power. After four days of misery, it was towed into Mobile, Ala. The more than 4,000 people on board had no showers, no modern sanitation, no air conditioning, makeshift food and sleeping arrangements. Many on board were terrified or horrified when their luxury vacation turned into a nightmare.

As I ponder that cruise ship lingering in the middle of the ocean with no power to reach land, I am struck with how we, on this planet, may become much like that cruise ship. "Triumph" had limited resources on board for the passengers. When a fire in the ship's engine room damaged the ship's generators and left it without electricity, the ability to handle modern appliances and conveniences disappeared. As the ship lingered in the ocean, trash and waste quickly accumulated until there was nowhere else for it to go. Portions of the ship became unsanitary and uninhabitable.

"Triumph's" generators can be replaced and its supplies restocked. But when the Earth's sources of usable energy and other natural resources fail, there will be no more. In the same way, whatever toxic waste we produce stays on this planet Earth and recirculates into our waterways and our air supply. It has even come to pollute the great oceans and kill wildlife in the middle of the Pacific.

If we can imagine ourselves living on Earth as those on that cruise ship, perhaps we will take better care of our planet. To do so, we need to understand the interconnectedness of our actions on the planet. Our climate is directly affected by our failure to be good stewards of the Earth. Our climate sustains life; destabilizing it has unforeseen consequences.

We cannot allow massive changes to take place through our negligence and believe we can carry on with our lives as usual. Climate is the broadest, deepest, and most intricate and vulnerable system on Earth. Climate can prohibit animals or human beings from occupying a formerly suitable habitat as floods may occur or the temperature may rise too high for vegetation or animals to survive. Global warming has demonstrated how vulnerable living creatures are to even a few degrees change in the Earth's average temperature.

No one can escape the effects of climate change: it does not discriminate against gender, ethnicity, status or nationality. With our fancy for comfortable and carefree lifestyles, we have contributed much to the world's pollution, which then affects our climate. Fossil fuels, coal, petroleum, and natural gas became the primary sources of energy with modern industrialization; burning them releases gaseous byproducts. Carbon dioxide is now 30 percent higher in the Earth's atmosphere than in preindustrial times; nitrous oxide is 19 percent higher.

In the 1970s, we began to realize that chemicals we use are causing holes in the ozone layer and allowing ultraviolet rays to penetrate the Earth. The damage is difficult to grasp because in our temperate zone, we don't see any strong influences of the change, but these chemicals affect the Earth and its inhabitants on different levels, many of which are still being discovered. Furthermore, pollution affects our clean water supply. More than 1 billion people have no access to clean drinking water. This means waterborne diseases afflict many. There is only so much water, land, and natural resources; if we don't give the Earth enough time to replenish the resources, and preserve enough woodlands to filter harmful chemicals, everything may be gone.

We have postponed our concern for the planet for too long. In the effort to acquire more goods, the Earth's resources are being destroyed as affluent people live in the illusion of unlimited resources while the rest of the Earth's people live in the reality of scarcity and want. The time to repent and reform is now. There is no time left for further denial or delay about global warming. The evidence of our changing climate has unmasked our denial, although large segments of Western culture have not yet accepted the need to adjust our lifestyles. Governments and industries are not eager to take the kind of action that is needed.

Perhaps, if we can all imagine ourselves living on that stranded Carnival cruise ship, we may begin to takes steps to live differently. Perhaps understanding that if we pollute our "ship" and use up all its resources, there will be no more left to keep us going. Unlike the Carnival ship, "Triumph," there are no other ships that can replace the "ship" we are on.

Reflection Questions:

1) How is the Earth like a cruise ship?
2) How does the Earth differ from a cruise ship?
3) How does understanding the Earth as a cruise ship challenge our current lifestyle of consumption?
4) What small steps can we take to start reversing the problems we have created and saving our planet?

14

Storms and the Environment

I HAD SUCH A terrible flu in early 2013 that I had no idea that snowstorm Nemo was predicted. However, when it hit, everyone in its path knew that Nemo had arrived. The snowstorm's path was similar to the track Hurricane Sandy took a few months earlier in October 2012. Those who were devastated by the hurricane now found themselves snowed in by Nemo. The beautiful, snow-filled pictures posted on social media belied the terrible damage the blizzard caused.

For people struggling to recover from Hurricane Sandy, Nemo dealt another blow to their capacity to rebuild their lives. With Nemo came at least nine reported deaths, 635,000 people without power, 38 inches of snow in some areas, and winds up to 75 mph in other places. It was a rough blizzard. Some people remained trapped in their homes for days, as no plough removal service could clear their driveways or the roads. Others went without power in temperatures much lower than when Sandy hit in the fall. Some people believe that these strange weather patterns and freakish storms are a statistical anomaly and everything will return to normal next year. But more of us are realizing that these climate changes result from our ways of living.

Storms and the Environment

There is a direct relation between our lifestyle, such as our desire for more material goods, and the environmental changes occurring all around us. Globalization and the strong desire for more material goods create polluting industries in countries with no strong anti-pollution legislation. We are creating new environmental problems by altering the global ecological balance.

In response, environmental leaders who are acutely conscious of the after-the-fact environmental problems caused by human endeavors (consequences not anticipated at the time of a project's inception) have proposed an environmental policy known as "the precautionary principle." This principle, already adopted by Germany and Sweden, establishes that if it is determined that a product or practice raises significant threats to human health or the environment, action may be taken to restrict, delay, or prohibit that product or practice.

This is a good principle to live by. Perhaps all the industrial countries should adopt the principle and put it into practice immediately. Individuals also should adopt this principle. If we learn that our actions harm the environment, we should consider twice before engaging in them. If every one of us makes small, positive changes in how we live, the impact can be huge on this planet. The starting point is to learn more about what kind of behavior is harmful to the environment.

We need to ask ourselves, how many more storms must we experience before we realize that we are part of this problem? How many more lives have to be lost before we change our habits and stop acting as if we can do whatever we wish on this planet without considering the consequences?

Storms will always seem to have a mind of their own, and storms will continue to take lives. But by following "the precautionary principle," we can be at peace knowing that we are not giving these monsters of weather any assistance. We need to remember that we only have one planet, one earth, and we need to take care of everything in it.

Reflection Questions:

1) We cause many of Earth's "natural" disasters. How can we live so we cause the least harm to the Earth?

2) What specific changes might you make to minimize your contribution to environmental harm?

3) If you applied "the precautionary principle" to your own life, what changes might you consider making?

4) In the Bible, God is said to be in control of the whole Earth even of the weather. Yet God has given humans a good deal of control on this planet, and our actions do have consequences. How do you think God's sovereignty and human freedom relate here?

5) Christians are called to be like Jesus. When it comes to helping those in need or praying for people, we heed the call quickly. But Jesus calmed a storm! What is our response to that? How should Jesus' actions then affect our actions now?

6) When there is a natural disaster Christians are often among the first to respond. We send food and workers to rebuild houses. These are all good things. But there is an old story of a man who kept pulling drowning kids out of a river. Eventually he decided to walk upriver and figure out why they were drowning in the first place. What can we do to get ahead of disasters, whether natural or human-created?

15

Consumption Overload

RECENTLY, I WATCHED A TV advertisement for a show on Oxygen called "My Shopping Addiction." As the title implies, it showcases people who have an addiction to shopping. I know of tobacco, alcohol, and drug addiction, but how can anyone be addicted to shopping?

Something doesn't seem right. Isn't this a simple matter of staying away from malls or online shopping websites? However, like other addicts, it is very difficult for shopping addicts to break their addiction. For some it has become "retail therapy." Some people spend thousands of dollars on brand-name purses, clothes and shoes. They are not the richest people, and many accumulate huge credit card debt.

As I go about my daily tasks, I can't keep from asking, "How did our society reach the point where people are addicted to shopping?"

We are constantly buying. It has now become a national pastime, a way of socializing, and a way of filling empty hours alone. We now have people from all over the world coming to the United States to buy cheap brand-name products. An entire commercial enterprise has developed around shopping tourism, flying individuals and groups directly to outlet malls and other shopping attractions.

Black Friday has practically become another national holiday. Every year leading up to this day and the Christmas season there are countless advertisements, announcing sales and discounts, all to feed our consumption lifestyle.

Theologians are beginning to examine our consumerist way of life. Shopping and consumption has become a new religion—and a dangerous one, too. For a larger and larger number of people, consumerism is the accepted and unquestioned way—the good way—to live and be in the world.

The new religion of consumerism in the Western world creates an allure about what we need, what we need to buy, how we are to live; we follow the tenets of this new religion unquestioningly. One good handbag deserves a dozen more. Consumerism has taken over our worldview and instructs us in how we are to act in this world according to our needs, our relationship to others, and the earth. It has even become the basis of our survival. As a consequence, we take too much from the earth without giving anything back or replenishing it. This life of consumerism will produce catastrophic results; it threatens our survival.

Consumerism is a civic religion that permeates our society; it is an obligation to feed our national gross domestic product and thereby attain a constant economic growth rate. Other faith commitments are less important. Consumerism has become a world religion and perhaps the most successful religion, in that it has slipped in under the radar, diminishing the surplus monies that may have been given as charity to those in need. People pay their tithes to this new religion by buying more than we can afford, blind to the consequences. We give our time, money, and energy to buy, hoard, and consume.

The "sanctuaries" of this religion are everywhere; there are 4 billion square feet of shopping space in the United States (16 square feet for every adult and child). This religion draws converts and proselytizes at a very fast rate. It attracts young people seeking meaning and fulfillment for their lives. The goal of this invisible religion is personal happiness. Acquiring "stuff" is the primary means to happiness. The words of American economist, Thorstein

Veblen from over 100 years ago still ring true today (I paraphrase) "...what good is money, if you can't show it off with goods."[3] Unfortunately, people wish to show off the goods even when they do not have the money.

Is the consumer society good for all? Not if some people go hungry while others live to excess. If all consume less, then the planet can support more; if some consume more, then others must consume less.

The commercial Christmas season, dedicated to the new religion of consumerism, is also the season of Advent for Christians when we remember the coming of God into our world (its where the word "Christmas" comes from, for goodness sake!). Before we attempt to clean out other people's houses we ought to start with our own. The church ought to take the lead in resisting the new god of consumerism who says you need more. We need the church to remind us that true human flourishing comes in following Jesus who gave up all.

Reflection Questions:

1) Think of what you consume during a day or a week. Identify some things you consume but do not truly need. Can you live on less?

2) Consumerism is built on the blood of other people, as far as half a world away. Our cheap goods often are made possible by the toil of our brothers and sisters in near slave-like working conditions. What do you know about where your goods come from? Are you willing to spend a bit more on fair trade products if you know it will help someone have a better life? What other strategies could you employ to consume more responsibly?

3) What ways can we celebrate birthdays and Christmas without buying into consumerism?

---

3. See Thorstein Veblen's 1899 book *Theory of the Leisure Class.*

16

Sustainability

Hurricane Sandy was worse than anyone imagined it would be. I saw countless images of terrible mayhem: I could barely believe the reports. I could not fathom that some homes burned down while sand and water buried others. One storm shattered countless lives. I kept viewing the pictures and the videos, which have a dream-like quality. I expected that I might wake up and find it was only a nightmare. But it wasn't.

The storm was real to thousands of victims. Sandy changed their lives in the short run by the effort and cost to rebuild, and in the long run by an apprehension of future weather disasters. I live in Pennsylvania where the damage was less than in New York and New Jersey. In our area, trees fell, roads flooded, siding flew off homes, and the power was off for three or more days, but these damages do not compare to those whose lives turned upside down.

As I look at the images and the videos of this storm, I keep wondering, "Could this happen again?" The answer is yes.

It was unfortunate that during the three 2012 presidential candidate debates, the important topic of climate change never came up. It was also nearly absent from the candidates' campaign speeches. Neither candidate wanted to mention the subject. The candidates focused on the economy or they felt the issue of

Sustainability

climate change was too technical, with too many opportunities to misspeak.

If we continue to ignore or dismiss the scientific reports of how our polluting, consumerist lifestyles and greed impact our environment, we will continue to eviscerate our planet. Scientists have warned us that global warming and pollution are leading to the possibility of catastrophic environmental events.

They have warned us that our pollution is creating and enlarging a hole in our upper atmosphere ozone layer at the north and south poles. This will melt our polar ice, increasing the sea level. This in turn will expose more water surface to the sun, which will increase atmospheric humidity, creating more frequent and more damaging storms. Meteorological trends lead me to believe Sandy is a precursor to more storms of comparable intensity and from unanticipated directions.

Eco-theologians such as Sallie McFague, Celia Deane-Drummond and Heather Eaton have warned us for close to 25 years about taking care of Earth. If we continue to consume the way we do, we will need to find four more planets to sustain our way of living. But we do not have four more planets. We have only one. We need to stop consuming resources solely for our selfish, short-term pleasure.

We must heed the warning of scientists who predict catastrophes and theologians who identify the selfish intent behind our way of life. Living by self-interest will overcome all of our agricultural advances and lead to planetary economic shortages comparable to the famines of biblical times. We need to stop misusing the land and start nurturing the forests and the oceans as a mother nurtures her children.

As Christians, we have failed to live out our God-given role as good stewards of the earth. We have taken advantage of every method imaginable to exploit the planet that God created and gave us to protect, nurture, and conserve. We have neglected God's commands to care for the earth. We have chosen primarily to exploit and deplete, as if we were playing some computer game where we could always restore a previous condition if we made a bad move. We have become greedy consumers with a pathological, unquenchable thirst for goods.

A storm like Sandy reminds us to become better parents to posterity and to take better care of the place that God has given to us. We cannot ignore this storm and go back to our old ways. As we clean up from this storm (and others to come), we need to remember that the economy is tied to global climate changes in eternal symbiosis. We therefore need our policy makers to take more seriously the concerns about our environment – or we need to make a point of electing those who will take these concerns seriously.

The less we care, the more problems we will create and leave behind for our children and grandchildren. I know we are smarter than that. Do we have the wisdom to listen to what we know? Let's not only clean up New York and New Jersey, let's clean up our act. Let's insure that humankind will flourish here on earth for generations to come.

Remember, our probes to Mars have yet to discover any "alabaster cities" or "amber waves of grain" on the red planet. Just dust, just like us, if we don't improve our care of the land.

Reflection Questions:

1) If we do not change our habits, we can destroy our world. How can we change our ways?
2) How can we start obeying God to take care of the planet?
3) What small steps is your family, church or community taking to help "clean up" our act?
4) What small steps can you add?

17

Pop Culture and Greed

THE MUSIC VIDEO "GANGNAM Style" is mesmerizing and addictive. It has lots of color, action, comedy, and variety. It is entertaining even if you do not understand Korean. Psy's video has drawn mass attention from Americans and others in the Western world to Korean popular culture. "Gangnam Style" has hit No. 2 on the U.S. Billboard chart. It now holds the Guinness World Record for "most liked" video. Before this success, Psy (Park Jae-sang) had been singing and performing for the past 11 years without any attention outside of Korea.

He has been well received in Korea since 2001, but in 2012 he broke out in Australia, New Zealand, Canada, Germany, Ireland, Norway, Switzerland, the United Kingdom and the United States. He appeared on "The Ellen DeGeneres Show," "Today," and "Saturday Night Live" among others. He continues to perform live concerts all over Korea.

Many ask, "Why all the crazy attraction now?" Sure, the music is upbeat; it is good for dancing and exercise. The video is entertaining and theatrical. However, there is something more that draws people to hear and watch "Gangnam Style." I think it is the message within the song.

I would say it is the subversive message of the song that keeps people watching, dancing, singing, reflecting and writing. What Psy does so cleverly in the fast-paced, entertaining song and music video is to provide a socioeconomic representation of rich people's lifestyle in Gangnam, Korea. Gangnam is a large, affluent district in Seoul, South Korea. It's smaller, relatively, than Manhattan, but larger than "midtown Manhattan."

Thirty years ago, Gangnam was the least developed part of Seoul. Now it is the most highly developed part of the city. The number of rich people residing in Gangnam, a neighborhood south of the Han River in Seoul, has skyrocketed. People in Gangnam live an opulent, over-the-top lifestyle: they dress in designer clothes, wear designer shoes and carry name brand handbags. The women tend to appear similar to one another with surgically enhanced faces and bodies. Residents drive expensive cars. Gangnam has become the most coveted address among Koreans as they strive for the symbols of affluence.

Gangnam, the district has become a microcosm for the rest of the world to examine, critique and evaluate. People around the world have seen what it means to live richly and they secretly desire a piece of that pie. The media has led them to believe that living that lifestyle will be fulfilling and enriching because it appears so for those who appear in advertising. Psy's video plays on the artificiality of this image. Psy ends up lying on a beach chair in a kid's playground instead of a beach. He doesn't ride real horses; he rides on a merry-go-round. When he walks with two beautiful women, they're not walking the red carpet; they're bombarded by trash.

Almost every scene is a critique of the lifestyle being celebrated in Gangnam. It isn't as wonderful and sumptuous as it is made out to be. Rather, it is lonely, meaningless, and worthless. Psy himself says in an interview about the making of his music video that it is all "hollow." What Psy is doing in this video is similar to what theologians have been proclaiming for the past 20 years as they have argued our consumerist lifestyle is empty and unfulfilling. We have made consumerism our new religion. We tithe at the mall and perform the weekly liturgy of "retail therapy." What seemed like an exciting thing to do has become a reflexive, zombie-like response. Filling our lives with material goods does not fulfill us or enrich us, so we need more.

Psy delivers a socioeconomic critique and does so in a catchy, playful way through "Gangnam Style." He does it with an infectious aesthetic that draws people's attention and makes them rethink their lives.

Perhaps theologians and pastors can learn from him and find different ways to reach out to the masses with the message to turn from our consumerist lifestyle to a lifestyle that seeks the Creator, not the created. Perhaps we can learn from Psy and make the turn on our own.

Reflection Questions:

1) Rather than dancing to the song of consumerism, what other songs can we dance to?
2) How is where you live like Gangnam in Korea? What sorts of things to people buy or possess to gain status in the eyes of others? Do you seek status from others in similar ways?
3) How is where you live different from Gangnam?
4) For every Gangnam there is a slum where people have nothing. Christians believe God is the creator of this world and all people are connected as they are made in God's image. Our choices to live an affluent lifestyle are connected to someone else's poverty. Do you agree? Why or why not? Has there ever been a time when this connection was made real to you in a concrete way?
5) There are many ways we can help others. One way is to sponsor a child through World Vision. Can you think of other ways?

18

Sustaining Life

GLOBAL SUSTAINABILITY HAS BECOME one of the most important issues in our time. In a hundred years, it may be the single most important issue. We have heard that if we do not sustain (a combination of conservation and renewal) our resources, we are on the road to a dystopia that would make a Hollywood scriptwriter cringe.

Winona LaDuke, a noted activist, author, and founder and codirector of Honor the Earth (www.honorearth.org) spoke on this issue at Moravian College in Bethlehem, Pennsylvania. LaDuke's words were powerful, empowering and enlightening. She emphasized the sacredness of the land and our intimate connection to the land. She provoked the crowd with the assertion that we can have a worldview that does not embody imperial ideas.

A society based on conquest is as unsustainable as the 19th-century notion of an economy based on constant colonial market expansion. There are no more productive lands to conquer.

LaDuke laid out some precepts for sustainability:

1. Understanding that the Creator's law is the highest law.
2. Understanding our relations to all who have paws, fins, legs, or roots

Sustaining Life

3. Understanding the cyclical patterns of nature.
4. Understanding that our deliberation needs to think about the consequences for the seventh generation into the future (in order to have any chance to survive on this planet for the next 1,000 years).

LaDuke criticized the United States, saying it emphasizes the understanding, "Man's laws are higher than Creator's laws." For example, she said that the number of pollutants in our biosphere depends on the politics of who is in office.

The United States treats pollution like a commodity and trades pollution credits. The interests of corporations, which suffer not one wit from pollution, are treated as if they were natural persons under the law. As in our modern myths, these inhuman surrogates destroy lands and leave little for our cousins. Despite what a notable quote from *Avatar* suggests, sooner or later the world will run out of trees.

LaDuke pointed out how Western culture thinks linearly. "West" is a state of mind, and we move to our frontiers with a view to their resources, which are valuable to us. We produce 70 trillion pounds of garbage; 70 percent of our economy is based on consuming things. We continue to waste water; we continue to waste people. Our linear economy is not sustainable as we continue to think only about quarterly profits and not about the cost in unrecoverable resources required to achieve those profits.

Americans are time conscious, LaDuke said, but we also have a bad case of amnesia. Based on current trends, by the year 2100, more than 50 species will have become extinct. That is a modest estimate. Dr. E. O. Wilson, a renowned biologist, has estimated that half of all species living today will become extinct by 2100 due to human effects on the biosphere. This is far higher than the pre-human extinction rate, where a species could expect to survive for about 10 million years. It is not about Darwin's natural course of events in nature; these figures are about our causing the sixth great extinction in the history of life on this planet. The evolutionary stem that produced *Homo sapiens* is about 4 to 8 million years old.

It would be tragic if we consumed ourselves into extinction before our normal time was up.

We have become addicted to energy and addicts do bad things and hang out with bad people. We cannot continue to consume one-third of the world's resources without replacing them. We need to think differently and develop sustainable solutions. We need to move from fossil fuel to renewable energy. We need to grow our own crops, build wind turbines and fight against hazardous nuclear waste dumps.

We need to think critically and be thoughtful and mindful. We need to stop converting a limited resource, petrochemicals, into a non-biodegradable waste. We must seek efficient uses and consume less. It often seems that Americans do not care, and we lack respect for the information we have. We cling to old values and ignore new facts. We lack faith in God's rule, while holding an unexamined faith that our supply of resources will never end and that nothing we can do will change our climate. Americans aware of the problem suffer from feeling powerless and respond to the problems with apathy, believing that the majority will never act on the prospect of their children's living on a desert world which will make the dystopian *The Road Warrior* or *The Book of Eli* look like a day at the beach. So the big question is, "How do we inspire people to care?"

This challenges me on a daily basis. How do I make my family, friends, students and community care about these issues and do something about them? LaDuke reminded us that democracy is not a spectator sport. We all need to participate and get involved in the work of sustainability. Change happens because we do something about it. We need to find some way of living that recognizes how all relatives live. The challenge is urgent. She also encouraged us all to dream big and think big: "If you are working on something that you plan to finish in your lifetime, you are not thinking big enough."

So the challenge rests on all of us who are part of God's reign here on earth. What will we do to help preserve the earth and make it more sustainable? It may involve taking small steps like using less water and natural resources.

Whatever it is, I hope that I can do my part. I hope we can each do our own part.

Reflection Questions:

1) How can we all be active and participate in sustainability?
2) How can we ensure that we do not destroy species and make them extinct?
3) How can we live faithfully and in harmony with all of God's creation?
4) How can we protect all our relatives-all the species with which we share God's creation
5) How can we participate in the democratic processes?
6) What is your dream for the future? How are you working on that dream?

Church and Society

19

Overcoming Racism and Building Bridges[4]

"It's so nice and warm on the inside that you forget that there's an outside. The worst of it is, the crab that mostly keeps you down is you... The realization had her mind on fire."

—Terry Pratchett, *Unseen Academicals*

I WAS HEADING HOME after speaking at a meeting of the Synod of British Columbia of the Presbyterian Church in Canada, when a short incident on the plane ended a wonderful and fruitful trip on a sore note. It was a long flight home from Vancouver to Philadelphia. My eleven-year old daughter, Elisabeth, and I had to get up at 5:00 am to catch an early morning flight. We left Vancouver around 7:00 am, transferring in Dallas to get to Philadelphia around 9:00 pm. It would be another hour drive before we reached home.

---

4. A similar version of this first appeared in *The Feminist Wire* under the title: "Yellow and White: Overcoming Racism." http://thefeministwire.com/2013/04/overcomingracism/ It is reused here with permission.

On the flight from Dallas to Philadelphia, my daughter and I sat in the second to the last row. An elderly white couple sat behind us. I have traveled enough to know the etiquette of deplaning. People in the first rows begin to move down the aisle, and everyone else waits their turn to follow. There are no choices. There is only one way out for everyone, unlike the numerous checkout lines at a supermarket or the double doors in a sanctuary.

We encountered a person who violated this rule when the plane opened its doors in Philadelphia due to an idea of racial superiority one would think had been erased from "polite society." We experienced more than thoughtlessness or rudeness. Thoughtlessness is simple oversight. Rudeness is asserting oneself in a situation just to feel a momentary state of power over another for example, edging ahead of someone else in a line, simply to get a better seat or a faster transaction. What my daughter and I experienced was more hurtful because it sent a clear message to us from that person: "I am better than you, I look down on you as a lesser human being."

As we got up from our seats and stood in place to enter the aisle, the white woman behind me stood next to me in the aisle and was determined to gain the place in the line ahead of me. Elisabeth was standing by her seat in the row beside me, and the woman's husband was standing behind us in the aisle.

We stood a long time, as it seemed to take longer than usual for the passengers ahead of us to file out of the passengers' cabin. When it became time for our row to exit, the elderly woman beside me started walking ahead and somehow got three rows in front of us. I am not sure how she managed that, but she did, leaving her husband behind us. So far, we have simple rudeness.

As she left the plane, the woman was well ahead of me. When it was my turn to walk out I asked her husband if he wanted to go ahead of us and catch up with his wife. He politely said, "Please go ahead." My daughter and I stepped from the passenger cabin.

As we emerged from the door ahead of her husband, a look of anger and disgust filled the woman's face. When we walked past her, she said aloud to her husband, "I can't believe you allowed the Chinese to get ahead of you!"

She spoke loudly enough so that I could hear. Her spiteful words hurt and angered me. My first thought was to remember how often Asian Americans are viewed as foreigners no matter how long they have been living in this country. Even fourth or fifth generation Asian Americans are viewed through stereotypes that reveal the historic and persistent racism experienced by this racial/ethnic group. Asian Americans have been depicted as "perpetual foreigners," "unassimilable," and other stereotypes. For example, almost every Asian American has experienced the "perpetual foreigner" syndrome. Many have been asked, "Where are you really from?" This loaded question differs from the usual one, "Where are you from?" The really-question figuratively and literally displaces the Asian American respondent back to Asia, because the assumption behind the question, even if the questioner is oblivious to it, is that Asian Americans can never be *from* or *of* the United States.[5]

Asian Americans, even if they are descendants of railroad workers who arrived in the middle of the nineteenth century, are assumed to be foreigners, while the white questioners, even if they are descendants of first generation immigrants, consider themselves as "true" Americans. Generally, there is no intention of offense, much less malice, on the part of a white questioner whose American identity would never be called into question. Nonetheless, the person who is asking the question brings to mind all the phrases that our "racialized society heaps upon Asian Americans: foreigner, unassimilable, not American, someone who simply does not belong in American society, or, to use the 'O' word, an 'Oriental.'"[6]

My second thought was that it did not matter so much that she failed to allow for the possibility that I was Korean (or Vietnamese or Thai or Mongol or Tibetan or Japanese) and not Chinese that bothered me. It was her tone and false understanding of

---

5. Please see Joseph Cheah, *Race and Religion in American Buddhism* (Oxford: Oxford University Press, 2011), 132.

6. Ibid., 132.

Asian Americans in general. In her mind, white people are entitled to go ahead of Asians Americans even if the simple logic of the queue says the Asian American should go first. This is comparable to the Jim Crow rule that said all African Americans must move to the back of the bus, thereby putting them behind all white Americans in the queue for disembarking. At many times and in many places, I have felt that communities around me act as if Jim Crow style laws are still *sub rosa* in effect for people of Asian heritage vis-à-vis Caucasian Americans. An Asian American can never remain ahead of a Caucasian, no matter what circumstances may have placed the Asian first.

This understanding and practice may not be as rigid as Jim Crow. Perhaps a better analogy is the discrimination against Jewish people described in the novel and film, *Gentleman's Agreement*[7]: a kind of discrimination that used all sorts of circumlocutions to hide the fact that it is taking place. There appears to be a glass ceiling that prevents Asian Americans from getting ahead as we are viewed as good, but not good enough to be at the top. But isn't that in some way a problem with how I feel more than what I experience?

Somehow, those of us who belong to a distinctly marginal class based on appearance are regarded as secondary human beings. It is not enough to simply look different. A cliché of the Western movie is that the down-on-his-luck white man, dirty and unkempt, is accepted while the clean, healthy Native American is rejected. Once people see members of a marginalized group as moving out of that secondary status or achieving more than our subordinate status dictates, we are often ignored or tagged as a reminder that we are a member of a disenfranchised race, nation, or people. One's "Asianness" signifies to the white dominant group that s/he is a foreigner. This is true even if one is a second, third, or fourth generation "immigrant." It is this racial difference, this physical difference of appearance, which marks Asian Americans as "other," and creates the status of "perpetual foreigner," which functions to marginalize

---

7. 1947 Novel by Laura Z. Hobson and film of the same year, starring Gregory Peck, directed by Elis Kazan.

Americans of Asian ancestry permanently. For women, it is even more complex: they have to endure both the patriarchal attitudes of their Asian ethnicity and those of their U.S. context.[8]

WHITENESS

My airplane incident is rooted in white privilege and how some members of society view race. Critical Race Theory emerged and evolved out of opposition to dominant conceptions of race, racism, and equality. What surfaced was a commitment to racial justice.[9] "Whiteness" shapes and constitutes mainstream U.S. culture and society. "Whiteness" is the ideology of calling people in the United States of different ethnicities (English, Irish, French, German, Italian, and so forth) who have somewhat fair skin, white. The purpose is not to find a common ethnic name for these people. Rather, white is actually a term of "ethnic erasure." The process of making groups "white" erases the different ethnicities and distinct histories of different group of people and blends them into one monolithic group as if their cultural differences do not exist.

This erasure makes the "white group" appear normal while other groups are considered below the norm. The term "white" creates a privileged group in relation to all "non-white" people. People who are different from the white group are considered ethnic, while the white group is not. Ethnic people belong to the "different," less normal group. Such categories should be viewed and used with suspicion, as it is usually those with power who get to do the labeling and naming.

Furthermore, this term "white" creates privileged groups in relation to all "non-white" people. The problem is the grouping

---

8. See Gale A. Yee, "Where Are You Really From? An Asian American Feminist Biblical Scholar Reflects on Her Guild" in *New Feminist Christianity: Many Voices, Many Views* edited by Mary E. Hunt & Diann L. Neu (Woodstock: Skylight Paths, 2010), 79.

9. See Jacqueline Battalora, "Whiteness: The Workings of an Ideology in American Society and Culture" p. 3–23, in *Gender, Ethnicity, and Religion: Views from the Other Side*, edited by Rosemary Radford Ruether (Minneapolis: Fortress Press, 2002), 3.

of a privileged group on the basis of a socially-constructed whiteness.[10] Therefore, whiteness needs to become visible as a racial construction. Whiteness shapes and constitutes mainstream U.S. culture and society, and seeks to develop ethical responses.[11] Thus, whiteness erases groups of different people with different ethnicities into one monolithic group as if their cultural differences do not exist.

"White privilege" is the outcome of a pervasive presumption of the racial superiority of whiteness.[12] White superiority is the presumption: white privilege is the material consequence. We need to renegotiate justice by making the privilege visible and dismantling it. To work towards a just society, it is necessary to dismantle social structures and replace them with an ideal of plurality, equality, and mutuality. This paradigm shift recognizes that there is a plurality of centers and embraces that plurality. Rather than searching for purity, we need to embrace "hybridity."

Race is not a social category that stands alone. It exists in dynamic interactions with gender, sexuality, and class. Yet race must be acknowledged as having been assigned such tremendous significance, both historically and today, in that it continues to provide unearned advantages to those racialized as white, albeit to varying degrees.[13] White privilege is so embedded in our culture and society, it is important to recognize this so that we can fight against it. The white woman on the plane sincerely believed that Asians are people who can be bypassed by white people, and therefore, even during the simple act of deplaning, she can barge ahead of me, as it is her right to do so under "white privilege."

My experience on that plane was rooted in the myth of white privilege, which allows the white woman to believe that she has

---

10. See Rosemary Radford Ruether, editor, *Gender, Ethnicity, and Religion: Views from the Other Side* (Minneapolis: Fortress Press, 2002), x, xi.

11. See Battalora, "Whiteness: The Workings of an Ideology in American Society and Culture," 3.

12. See *Tim Wise: Anti-Racist Essayist, Author, and Educator* (www.timwise.org).

13. Ibid., 10–13.

every right to discriminate against a person of color and that she can get away with it.[14] Acting out of her privilege, the woman ignored the diversity of Asia and picked "Chinese," the largest Asian population in the U.S.

FINAL THOUGHTS

This plane incident has been quite painful to me, especially since I did not experience it alone. My young daughter also had to experience first-hand the humiliation of being dismissed on the basis of our skin color. That moment on the ramp leading from the plane reminded me that racism is so deeply embedded in our culture and we need to take steps to dismantle it.

I am not sure why the disposition to demean some other people based on racial background still exists and permeates much of our society. The ignorance or lack of respect for people with differences becomes visible in many aspects of our lives. However, we need to move beyond treating each other differently because of the color of our skin or the shape of our eyes or the size of our noses. We need to celebrate overcoming the evil influence created by a viral perception of differences that are before us rather than being fixated on them and allowing them to come between people.

I envision a world for my daughter in that people of all races, ethnicities, sexual orientations, and social classes can come together in harmony and love. My daughter's world should be free of hatred, racism, sexism and other "isms." Each one of us can work toward it and try to help it happen.

Reflection Questions:

1) When did you first become aware of racism? What happened? How did the important people in your life help you understand the experience?

---

14. See Joseph Cheah, "Race and Religion in American Buddhism" (Oxford University Press, 2011).

2) How is racism played out in your own life or community? Think of your own encounters with racism, whether you benefited from white privilege or experienced racism from others. How have such experiences changed you?

3) Those who have privilege often do not know it until someone points it out to them. How have you experienced privilege? How have you been privileged due to your race, gender or something else? What do you think is the best way to overcome privilege?

4) How do we work to dismantle racism? How can we start building a better society?

20

Peace on Earth and Gun Violence

WHEN CHRISTIANS CELEBRATE CHRISTMAS, we want to take a moment to pause and reflect upon what it means.

As we live through the busyness of getting into the Christmas spirit, the message of the birth of Christ may become lost in the fervor of buying presents, decorating the trees, and preparing festive dinners. In the midst of all the craziness of the holiday season, the theological significance of how Christ is connected to peace may become lost even to those following him.

We live in a society that accepts a much higher rate of violence, especially violence using firearms, than other countries do. This disturbs our ability to find peace in our everyday lives. On December 14, 2012 the unspeakable happened: 20 children and 6 adults were gunned down at Sandy Hook Elementary School in Newtown, CT. On December 21, 2012 people across the nation paused for a moment of silence at 9:30 a.m. to remember those whose lives were taken away so quickly and so senselessly.

In wake of such tragedy, how can we experience peace? How is the message of Christ's peace to the world to be welcomed by people who fear violence and tragedy? Where is peace when what happened at Sandy Hook can happen in our community and neighborhood?

Many remain horrified by the shooting of children at Sandy Hook Elementary School. Eight similar attacks occurred in 2012. As of September 2013, less than a year after Sandy Hook, a little more than 10 000 people had been killed by guns in the U.S. The unthinkable happened again and again and the world stands stunned and speechless. We mourn as a community, a nation, and the world.

As I think about the terror of such shooting events, I cannot help but wonder how we can be agents of peace. How can we bring peace into our world where there is so much violence and tragedy? What could we have done to prevent the horror that happened at Sandy Hook Elementary School?

I recall watching an interview of Rep. John Lewis on MSNBC soon after the Sandy Hook shooting. A U.S. Representative, Lewis has served Georgia's 5th congressional district since 1987. One of the Big Six leaders in the American Civil Rights Movement, Rep. Lewis chaired the Student Nonviolent Coordinating Committee (SNCC), playing a key role in the struggle to end legalized racial discrimination and segregation.

Because of his prominent leadership, Rep. Lewis has spoken out on many civil rights issues. In the interview I saw, he was being asked about gun control and the tragedy that occurred at Sandy Hook Elementary School. Lewis replied, "I cried. . . .. I cried all day." He understood the pain of losing lives shortened by gun violence.

Lewis also understood that the children did not have to die in this senseless and tragic way. When asked about stricter gun laws, Rep. Lewis responded: "The British are not coming." He recognized that things are not the same in America as they were in the days of the Revolution and the War of 1812.

Things have changed. We need to reexamine our gun laws and understand that they are causing more pain than protection. Gun violence tears up families, friends, communities, and the country. It is difficult to say one thing can help build a more peaceful society. However, stricter gun laws can only help bring more peace to this country. Many countries around the world, such as Australia, have enacted strict gun laws, and they appear to have

Peace on Earth and Gun Violence

worked. We need to act now. For too many families, now is already too late.

Reflection Questions:

1) What if anything, makes you nervous to think and talk about gun violence?

2) Guns are everywhere in our culture. Children play first-person-shooter video games where the body count multiplies; billboards for gun shows litter our highways; and hunters take to the woods each year to bring back a meal. What is your experience with guns? How has your experience, your view or perception of guns and gun violence changed?

3) How has gun violence touched your life?

4) What are some practical steps to take to work towards ending gun violence?

5) What steps can we take to become peacemakers in a violent world?

21

Churches around the World

MANY MAINLINE DENOMINATION CHURCHES, such as the Lutherans, Presbyterians, Episcopalians, and Methodists, struggle to survive in North America. Grim statistics reveal a decline in mainline Protestant church membership. For example, the Evangelical Lutheran Church in America began with 5.2 million members in 1987. In 2011, it had 4 million members. Congregations close or merge in many parts of the country. Seminaries struggle to cope with lower enrollment. Ironically, attendance in the Roman Catholic Church in the U.S. is increasing but there is an acute shortage of priests.

The future of the church may be glum in North America, but this is not the reality in other parts of the world. In his book *New Faces of Christianity*[15], Philip Jenkins outlines the reality of church growth in Africa, Asia, and South America, noting how the church is moving to the Global South.

We in Europe and North America must learn from the Global South to understand how we can revitalize the church life in our regions. To this end, it is encouraging to see groups like the World

---

15. Philip Jenkins, *New Faces of Christianity* (New York: Oxford University Press, 2006)

Council of Churches (WCC) work with congregations all over the world to make a positive impact.

The WCC is an ecumenical organization founded in 1948 that is committed to much of the work of the church and various church organizations. Three of the WCC's assembly commitments are to Pentecostalism, bringing the church's concerns and voice to the wider society, and working toward economic justice.

First, the WCC recognizes that Pentecostalism is a key ecclesial reality today. Pentecostalism is about self-giving and renewal through personal experience of God. It is an important ecclesial reality. The Pentecostal church is an ecumenical movement, and the WCC needs to see its role in the international arena. It is Pentecostal churches whose membership is either stable or growing in the United States.

Second, the WCC brings the churches' concerns and voice to the wider society. The council's struggle is to work for human justice, and the WCC seeks to lead in the struggle for human justice. The WCC has the advantage of being able to work with international organizations. Compared to individual churches, this organization of churches does not have to be burdened with dogmatic affirmations and can work with dynamism to examine human rights issues.

Third, the WCC expresses a deeper concern for economic justice. The WCC recognizes that the growing economic gap between countries, peoples, and classes is one of the world's most serious problems today. The WCC wants to narrow the economic gap and move in solidarity with the poor. The WCC's 10th Assembly will meet in Pusan, Korea, from October 30 to November 8. 2013 with the theme, "God of Life, Lead Us to Justice and Peace."

Korea is a unique country as it is the only one in the world still divided into two different governments. In 1945, in the aftermath of World War II, the Soviet Union and the U.S. agreed on the surrender of the Japanese forces that had occupied Korea since 1905. This left Korea partitioned along the 38th parallel, with the North under Soviet occupation and the South under U.S. occupation. These circumstances soon became the basis for the shaping of Korea by the two superpowers. The Soviet Union and the U.S. established governments centered on their respective ideologies, leading to Korea's division into two political entities: The Democratic People's Republic of Korea (North) and The Republic of Korea (South).

As we think about this divided country, we need to keep Korea in our prayers and to reflect upon what it means to have peace in this world. As the WCC assembly meets, we need to pray for God's peace as we think about the churches in Korea. My hope is that the churches can work for peace following the WCC assembly in Pusan.

We need to work for justice and reconciliation between the halves of this divided nation, so that it can be one country again. We need to motivate political and religious leaders to work toward illuminating those who can make this happen and create partnerships with the major players, such as China, Russia, Japan, and the U.S. We need to work toward encouraging our young children and youth to work toward justice and political liberation.

We need to work toward achieving human rights for the people of North Korea. One person's suffering under injustice is an injustice for all people, just as any benefit achieved for the least of God's people is done for God.

Reflection Questions:

1) How are churches to survive when there is so much disinterest and decline in the church?

2) We need to strengthen our churches by building better communities and places to love one another. How can we begin to do this in our own communities?

3) How do you participate in strengthening the mission of the church?

4) What do you know about Korea and the church in Korea? What would you like to learn?

22

Reimagining Society

MUCH OF MY PERSONAL life occurs where race, religion, and gender issues intersect. In some ways, the word *intersect* is too gentle. Perhaps *collide* better captures what occurs in my life as an Asian North American woman theologian, writer, minister, and mother. As I try to engage in theological dialogue, live in community with the dominant, unfamiliar culture, and raise my children to be just in this world, I realize that the lives of all people, especially people of color, collide and clash with others on the critical issues of race, religion, and gender.

Due to such clashes and collisions on critical issues, it is important that scholars of color come together to discuss new ideas, concepts, and thoughts on handling such encounters. This was the vision of my friends Dr. Miguel De la Torre (Iliff School of Theology), Dr. Stacey Floyd-Thomas (Vanderbilt), and Dr. Anthony Pinn (Rice University), who had the foresight to begin such a forum in the *Society of Race, Ethnicity and Religion (SRER)*. They recognized that scholars of color are doing important scholarship that should not be ignored by the wider academy. Scholars of color must continue to work with each other to express concerns, issues, and the importance of scholarship from the different perspective of the minoritized, as well as to continue working through mainstream journals, classes, schools, and professional societies. Solidarity must be reaffirmed and encouraged. The cross pollination of scholarship must be encouraged, and a venue created where peer review of scholarship by theologians of color is done by true peers.

This new society is bursting with potential. I did not know what to expect from the inaugural meeting that was held in Chicago, April 26–28, 2013 at the Lutheran School of Theology at Chicago and McCormick Theological Seminary. I did not know if many people would attend, what type of scholarship would be shared, and how people would accept the scholarship. Due to these uncertainties, I decided to send a very "safe" paper proposal in response to the theme for the meeting: "State of Our Union." What I mean by a "safe" proposal is that I submitted a paper that does not deal with racism.

I can write about racism in books, articles, chapters, and columns, but to talk about it in front of an audience or class is very difficult to me. It is difficult because it is so personal. I have experienced racism throughout my life. Now as a mother, it is also difficult to experience racism in front of my children and see my children experience it.

I realize the personal can become political and I recognize that it is important to address racism. It takes courage publicly to talk about racism. It takes courage because the act of engaging racism entails letting go: letting go of comfort and entering into the wilderness of "unknowing." It opens the door for criticism, hostility, and opposition. You never know what kind of interpersonal land mines you may touch off by colliding with the opinions of some members of your audience.

Taking steps to talk about racism publicly also involves "reimagining." To me, reimagining implies taking a risk to make a mistake, a risk to lose what one believes, and a risk to feel betrayed by one's people. Reimaging also involves openness to change. This involves being open to the transformative power of the Spirit, not unlike the spirit of *kenosis* described in Philippians 2:6–10. The change may involve changing one's course and one's personal perspective. When this happens, there may be an element of surprise, wonder, and astonishment.

So instead of taking risks and having the courage to do a paper on racism, I decided to give a paper on "Sustainability and Han." It was a paper on eco-justice and the suffering of the earth and its people. It was a safe paper because it focuses on a familiar topic among theologians on the margins.

However, as each presenter went before me, they addressed racism and/or shared their personal experiences about racism. The presenters were passionate and they were courageous in sharing their personal stories of racism.

As I heard each presenter speak, I recognized that this society was a safe place to discuss delicate topics such as racism, white privilege, white supremacy, and other structural "isms." Perhaps, I should have taken the risk. Perhaps I should have "let go" and begun the journey towards "reimagination." If I had done this, my personal reality would have become political. My personal concern may have encouraged others to take a risk. Doing so may help us take action so we can all help one another along this difficult journey to rectify the injustices in our society and country and to create a better world for our children and the generations to come.

As we think about our children, it is imperative not only to write about the problems of racism, but also talk about them so we can work towards eliminating racism. In addition, as we also work towards a more equal society for both men and women, we also need to talk about male privilege, male supremacy, and related structural "isms." We need to engage in dialogue and perhaps live by the words of Martin Luther King, Jr., who stated, "Our lives begin to end the day we become silent about the things that matter."

Reflection Questions:

1) When did you find yourself touched and moved by sisters and brothers who courageously shared their stories? What happened?

2) How do we find the courage to address racism and other structural "isms" and make our society a better place to live?

3) How do we reimagine a society that helps us in our daily work to rebuild each other and ourselves?

23

God and Politics

I WILL NEVER FORGET the answer George W. Bush gave in an early presidential primary season debate on December 13, 1999, when asked to name his favorite political philosopher. He looked into the camera and, with a child-like demeanor, said, "Jesus Christ, because he changed my life." I didn't know whether to laugh or cry.

Bush's answer opened up the discussion of how religion and American politics are intertwined. American politics shows how differing political opinions influence religious decisions and differing religious confessions influence (or are used to validate) political values.

I am Canadian. I grew up in Canada. Most of the people who run for Prime Minister are Protestant or Roman Catholic. Many of them are religious and attend Sunday worship service. However, religion and politics do not mix in Canada, where much political thought is influenced by its being an officially bilingual country. If a candidate for Prime Minister talked about God on the campaign trail, Canadians would believe the candidate is strange or has become a little crazy. A candidate who talked about God would likely lose the opportunity to become the Prime Minister.

It is the opposite in American politics. Presidential candidates believe they often have to talk about God, refer to God, and describe how God is viewed by their faith and therefore in their politics. As the 2012 Vice Presidential debate between Joseph Biden and Paul Ryan demonstrated, this means they must even speak to the issue if their point is that their religion has no influence on their politics. Both Vice President Biden and Mr. Ryan are Catholic but the two have very different views on the influence of faith and politics.

Despite that moment, the 2012's election campaign has seen relatively little "God-Talk." It is usually the conservative right who like to push the God-talk upon the candidates to demonstrate which candidate is "more" Christian than the other. Parties frequently use Christianity or God-talk on the campaign trail to sway voters and convince them that one candidate is the better Christian than the other. Or they paint the false picture that the other candidate isn't even Christian at all. Much religious talk and some phony issues revolve around the character of the candidates. The ink spilled and sound bites spoken over President Obama's birthplace and Mr. Romney's tax returns are less about substance than they are about whether or not the candidate is lying.

Mitt Romney was usually shy to talk about God, but once in a while he went off script and brought God back into the conversation. In reaction to the Democratic Party that had to argue to get God back into its platform at the convention, Mr. Romney said, "I will not take God out of my heart, I will not take God out of the public square, and I will not take God out of the platform of my party."

However, Mr. Romney still avoided discussing his own faith conviction and what it means for him to believe in God. Since Mr. Romney is a Mormon, a minority religion[16], possibly not even truly Christian, he had a difficult time with that issue. The conservative right commentators also shied away from religion, God-talk and Christianity.

The presidential candidate who can sincerely and genuinely talk about God will attract the voters, because regardless of their faith, an honest faith stance demonstrates a positive character. This worked well with Jimmy Carter. However, to use God and

---

16. Scholars often tend to categorize the Church of the Latter Day Saints as the fourth Abrahamic religion, after Judaism, Christianity, and Islam.

God's name to sway voters is simply manipulation. It puts voters off, because it is no longer a matter of personal conviction, it becomes a matter of "you must do what I believe." This is poison, especially in regard to social issues such as feminist matters and the environment.

Furthermore, having faith does not merely mean "talking about God" but is about "living out the gospel and showing God within our lives." We all know that actions speak louder than words. If a candidate cannot live out the faith, but can only "talk about God" it means nothing. "Faith without deeds is dead" (James 2:26). Living out the gospel means obeying God's commandment to love God and to love your neighbor as yourself. This includes taking care of the poor, the elderly, the widow, the distraught, and the downtrodden. When a candidate merely "talks" about their faith without wanting to live out the gospel, it makes voters wonder which God the candidate believes in.

As we reflect upon elections and who to vote for, we should remember that using the name of God to manipulate an election does not reliably reveal anything about the candidate's beliefs or faith in God. It reminds me of the commandment, "Do not use the name of God in vain" (Exodus 20:7). It also reminds us of the command, that "when you do it to the least of these, you have done it to me" (Matthew 25:40).

Reflection Questions

1) How can we engage in our faith and also in our civic duties?
2) How do we recognize integrity in candidates for office? What roles do the integrity of candidates play as you decide about how you will cast your vote?
3) In a political landscape fraught with turmoil, name-calling and rhetoric that claims one side is all right and the other is all wrong, how do we represent God faithfully? How do we speak the truth when it may get us in trouble from both sides?

24

Acting on Injustice

CAPE TOWN, SOUTH AFRICA, is one of the most stunning places I have visited. The landscape is unforgettable: mountains, blue waves, pristine beaches, and rich soil.

Juxtaposed to the land's beauty, however, are townships that provide an ugly reminder of the apartheid past. I visited Khayelitsha Township in Cape Town, and it was like time had stood still in that place.

The world has heard of the end of apartheid. We have heard of the political ascendancy of the African National Congress and of the election of Nelson Mandela and several successors to the presidency. We have heard about a New South Africa. This makes it all the more astonishing to see the poor, unsanitary living conditions of the black South Africans in the townships.

They live in tiny shacks put together with scrap materials. The roofs of these homes usually leak during the rainy season, so it may be days before inhabitants get to sleep on something dry. There are also communal bathrooms that the government built throughout the township: one toilet shared by many homes. With no indoor plumbing, the people have to leave their shacks to get water. Water pumps dot the township.

Acting on Injustice

The townships that exist today give the impression that apartheid has never been dismantled. And we ask ourselves: How is it possible that such an evil system has been eliminated yet millions of black South Africans live in such wretched conditions? How does this mistreatment of people of color relate to our preconceived notions of who others are?

The black Africans were the natives of southern Africa. The Dutch and the English colonized and dominated the country. The power that a few white people, especially when backed by force of arms, had over people of color was astounding.

Unfortunately, this process of discrimination and denomination is partially rooted within Christianity and partially with the ways in which religions develop and maintain the status quo in many situations. Furthermore, some among the small percentage of black Africans who have gained power and money have in some ways contributed to maintaining the status quo. This is the unfortunate nature of humanity, which fails to recognize the necessity to change the system so that all, not only a few, are liberated. From a religious point of view, the racism and prejudice that exist in Christianity can be associated with a particular strain of Dutch Calvinism.

The Dutch Calvinist Afrikaners contended that God had made a special covenant with them, a covenant that essentially gave them a "Promised Land" and excluded the indigenous population. This is virtually identical to the picture presented in Joshua and Judges. The Israelites were promised Canaan; however, to take that land, they had first to evict the tribes of the Canaanites. The distortion of Christianity here is the pretension that God has specially elected a particular ethnic or racial group at the expense of others, something Calvin himself would have found incomprehensible.

This grave misinterpretation formed within the Christian thinking and psyche to confirm and reconfirm racism within religion and Christianity. Dutch Calvinism is one example: there are many other examples of racism that has been imbedded into religion to make it appear as some divine doctrine that all followers must abide by, that some people can be saved and others cannot.

This type of Christian doctrine and belief is outrageous. It is mindless irreverence and heresy. However, such thinking continues to exist within our culture. A contemporary version says: people who make money are saved, those who do not, aren't. If we do not do anything about this thinking, then we are part of the problem. We see injustice within our society, culture and our churches. But if we do nothing, we make it worse. The question is how do we eliminate this oppression and achieve justice? We are all part of the community of creation. Shalom needs to be let loose, and we need to restore the world and work toward justice.

Prayer: Almighty and Everlasting God, who art always more ready to hear than we to pray, and art wont to give more than either we desire, or deserve: Pour down upon us the abundance of thy mercy: forgiving us those things whereof our conscience is afraid, and giving us those good things which we are not worthy to ask, but through the merits and meditation of Jesus Christ, thy Son, our Lord. Amen. *(The Book of Common Prayer)*

Reflection Questions:

1) What examples of social injustice do you see today? How do they function?
2) How are we each part of the social injustice within our society?
3) How can we work towards eliminating social injustice?
4) How do you envision the Reign of God? How do you seek to live into that Reign?

25

Working through Racism

Puerto Rico is a beautiful island with lakes, rivers, mountains, rainforests, and of course picturesque beaches. I received a warm welcome at the San Juan airport: 92 degrees with 74% humidity. Despite the hot, humid weather conditions, I went with eagerness to explore the culture, history, and tradition of Puerto Rico and reflect upon theological education in light of Hispanic theology.

This beautiful island was home to 70 seminary students for two weeks as they took courses through the "Hispanic Summer Program" (June 16–29, 2012). In addition, 10 faculty teachers and administrators participated in "Through Hispanic Eyes," a four day "mini program" for non-Hispanic faculty. I was one of them.

We visited classes and spoke with the Hispanic faculty members who shared their own struggles and how this program helped them. Our group leader was Dr. Luis Rivera-Rodriguez, who is the James G.K. McClure Professor of Theological Education, Dean of the Faculty, and Vice President for Academic Affairs at McCormick Theological Seminary. He was both informative and caring, which helped us explore some of the various issues that Hispanic students and faculty face during their seminary experience. We had deep and thoughtful discussions regarding white privilege, tokenism, and academic and cultural racism.

White privilege is prevalent in our society and in our seminary classrooms. Not only do students of color have to overcome the negative aspects of white privilege, so too the professors. As theological educators, the question of erasing white privilege is an ongoing concern as it brings an extra layer of unwelcome dynamic within the classroom. Many seminaries do not want to tackle this difficult problem; therefore the question of white privilege is ignored or pushed to the margins. In many ways, seminaries become blind to the issue of white privilege within the classroom and the institution.

Different countries deal with ethnic minority issues in various ways. I grew up as a Korean immigrant in Canada. Canada is a land of immigrants, where people from all over the world come to live. In Canada, the term used by governments for "people of color" is "visible minorities." I grew up knowing and internalizing that somehow I was a "visible minority." But what does it mean to be "visible" and a "minority." In some ways, this term labeled me as someone who "stands out" in a crowd. My face and body became racialized by a society that did not want to accept me as "normal." The irony is that, even though I was labeled a "visible minority," I become invisible when it came to issues of race, ethnicity and religious heritage.

When I reflect upon the colonization of Puerto Rico, I cannot help linking the idea of "visible minority" to how Puerto Rico as viewed by the United States. It is a territory of the U.S. with Commonwealth status that reduces its power of self-government. Puerto Ricans are allowed to vote during the U.S. primaries but not during the U.S. general elections. Puerto Rico has been used by the United States to produce cheap goods for Americans in the fifty states. Thus in many ways Puerto Ricans have become a "visible minority" whose real problems, struggles and dreams have been ignored or erased.

As we bring this back into our classrooms, we must not make the "students who are members of racialized minorities" within the classroom invisible. We cannot ignore their issues. We must move forward and work for a theological education style and system that will invite and include all people. Theological education needs to identify and erase "white privilege" within our classrooms and seek diversity, intercultural, and multi-contextual ways of learning and teaching so that all those whom God calls are valued equally.

Reflection Questions

1) White privilege has been destructive to our society. How can we work to eliminate white privilege and to build a just society?

2) How have you seen white privilege, or other forms of privilege, at work in our schools? How have you seen them in the workplace? How have you seen them in other settings? What changes need to be made to empower all people?

3) If you are a white person reading this, you may bristle at the idea of "white privilege." Your reaction may be that you have worked hard to get what you have, that you view and treat all people equally. The thing about privilege though is that those with it do not notice it. Now that you know about it, if you take an honest look at your life, can you see where privilege may have helped you? What can you do to help others who are not privileged?

4) If you are someone who has been the victim of the privilege of others, you may desire revenge or to get even. It is valid to be upset, but the goal is not simply to remove one group of privileged people and replace them with another. The goal is to create a world where everyone has equal opportunity. Are there people you resent and refuse to work with? How might this harm building a future, better world? Who do you need to forgive? How can you extend that forgiveness?

26

Teaching Race in School

MY THREE CHILDREN WENT back to school, as they always do in September. Now I can't get the song, "It's the Most Wonderful Time of the Year" out of my head, and it isn't even Christmas!

My children spent a lot of the summer at home (when we were not travelling), so it is wonderful to have them back at school. I started counting the weeks, days and hours before they returned to school... in June!

Like many moms in America, I keep my children busy throughout the year. They belong to sports teams, go to music lessons, attend Korean school, and engage in other extra-curricular activities. I sign them up for as many things as we can afford and as we have the time to drive them back and forth. It adds up to a lot of activities. Sometimes it feels like the children are running from one activity to the next. Things got so crowded that when my youngest son was in second grade, he returned from a hard day at school and demanded, "Why did you have to sign me up for school, too?"

School is not an option for children. They must attend school and try to get the best possible education. However, when I examine some of the traditional curricula of primary (elementary) schools, there are important topics that are missing. History and literature courses could teach our children about the nature of racism, sexism, and privilege. Books that quickly come to mind as resources, suitable for fifth and sixth grade, might be *Huckleberry Finn*, *Oliver Twist*, and *Alice in Wonderland*.

These problems of racism, sexism, and privilege are woven into the social fabric of our society, and these three 19th Century stories indicate that the problems are chronic. It is important for children to understand these issues and how we are to live in peace and good faith with one another.

Racism is a problem in our North American society. It promotes domination of the weakly enfranchised by a privileged group in the economic, social, cultural, and intellectual spheres.[17] Racism is so embedded in our society that, like a virus, when federal laws ban it, it mutates into forms with hidden symptoms, harder to demonstrate in courts. As long as parents neglect to teach our children about racism, it will be sanctioned in the minds of those who inherit the power of the vote and the power of the dollar.

As an Asian American woman and an immigrant from Korea to Canada to the United States, I have experienced racism. I battle racism on different fronts and try to bring it from the shadows to reveal it as the anti-Christian reality that it is. Racism confronts people of color and produces discrimination, to which the people often react with frustration and anger. Due to racism, it is difficult to join the dominant culture, which exacerbates alienation. Asian Americans feel an invisible boundary that prevents our belonging to the mainstream culture at work, school, or community. Racism and cultural separatism have set up walls that Asian Americans cannot seem to climb. This has been a constant struggle for me and it will remain one as long as a dominant race maintains the ability to hire and promote. Therefore it is necessary that we all work together to remove these barriers by equalizing power among all segments of society.

Racism leads to marginality. Marginal people live in between places. Immigrants belong fully to neither their native culture nor

---

17 [17]Fumitaka Matsuoka, *The Color of Faith: Building Community in a Multiracial Society* (Cleveland: United Church Press, 1998), 3.

to the host culture. The best examples are the ghetto-like neighborhoods in older cities such as the Italian, Jewish, Russian, Muslim, Irish, German, Chinese, and Hispanic enclaves in New York City, Philadelphia, Boston, Baltimore, and San Francisco.

We dwell in two places belonging to neither one nor the other. This creates a marginality that reinforces the inclination to stay in a ghetto society. This, in turn, creates feelings of hopelessness, pain, and subordination. It creates limitations as people try to overcome these barriers at the same time as we continue to feel safe behind them. The good news is that many older ghettos have been subsumed into the city or are literally disappearing, the way the NYC Italian neighborhood around Mulberry Street is being folded into the surrounding Chinese neighborhood.

Since racism has gone underground after the battles of the 1960s, it must be taught and brought out into the light. If it goes unchecked or unchallenged, it will continue to perpetuate prejudice, discrimination, and white privilege. This will have negative effects on all of society. This issue needs to be addressed at an early age. Children need to be able to understand, tackle, and overcome this barrier in society. They need heroes and models who look like them, and they need to see them from the very beginning of life. Children must understand their own pride, and the ways racism is an acid that erodes that pride. The Irish and the Italians and now the African-Americans have their cultural heroes recognized by the whole country. All races need to see their leaders standing side-by-side, free of discrimination, condemning discrimination, and vilifying discriminators. And, in order to do that, the teachers of children must be taught how to handle this subject.

The younger we start adding these important matters to our school curriculum, the better society that we can build. The better society we can maintain, the closer we come to building the reign of God in this world. Let us dream together and envision a society that will accept all people regardless of race, ethnicity, and gender.

Reflection Questions:

1) How do we introduce the conversation of race and racism to our young school children?
2) How do we set examples of kindness, goodness, and love rather than discrimination, judgment, and prejudice to our young children?
3) How do we help to build healthy, loving children?
4) Who were your heroines, heroes, and role models when you were a child? How do you share a diverse group of role models with children?

27

Immigration

I CAN ONLY IMAGINE how terrifying and difficult it was for my mother to bring her two little girls on a plane, via Alaska and Hawaii, finally to arrive at the Toronto Pearson Airport only to find that my father was not there to greet or pick us up. As usual, he was late. It was January 17, 1975 when we emigrated from Korea to Canada. My father had already left Korea a month earlier.

Growing up, my mother did not have the privilege of a higher education as her family was poor and she had seven siblings. She grew up during the aftermath of the Korean War when life was extremely difficult. In Korea, if families had any extra money, they educated the boys before the girls. I can only imagine the anxiety and trepidation she must have felt as she boarded a plane for the first time in her life and left Korea, without understanding a word of English and not knowing what future awaited her in a new foreign land.

I still remember that day we left Korea. My grandmother (*chin-hal-muh-nee*) told me that the flight would be very long and there were no restrooms on the plane. So she made me sit in the bathroom for a very long time so that I would not have to go again until I arrived in Canada. I remember my uncle (*keun-ah-buh-gi*) giving my sister and me each a very pretty necklace (which I still have) with personal information written on the back of the pendant in case we got lost. I remember being in the airport with my mother and sister and our uncles, aunts, and cousins who came out to say their goodbyes. My sister and I carried very big red bags that my aunts called "immigration bags" as we flew across the Pacific to an unknown land. Every one of our family members wept, especially my grandmother. They thought they would never see us again.

Since I was only five, I didn't realize the impact that day would have on the rest of my life. My mother was only twenty-nine and did not know what was waiting for her as she left Korea. She left her entire family to join my father since it was his idea to leave Korea against all the wishes of his family. She left behind everything she had known: her family, her house, her community, her friends, her culture, and her history in order to start afresh in a new and foreign land. I can only imagine the fear in her heart as she obeyed my father. As many first generation immigrants can remember, it was not easy to make a new start in a new place. It was not a "land of milk and honey" as everyone had told them it would be. Rather, it was a hard, and sometimes a heart-wrenching, life.

We landed in Toronto in January during one of the harshest winters in Canada. We were so cold and miserable that I remember wanting to stay indoors all day long. I started kindergarten and remember being mocked by other children who did not know "what" I was. Many Canadians kept asking me if I were Chinese or Japanese. When I told them I was Korean, they said, "What is Korean? You can't be Korean. You are Chinese or Japanese (and other terms were used to describe me)." With my lack of English, I was a constant target of racism. I can only imagine the frequent regret my mother must have felt when she experienced extreme isolation, loneliness, and a sense of hopelessness as she tried to adjust to a foreign land that did not welcome her or her family. She endured in silence the racism and sexism that she faced. She never openly shared her pain even though it was visible on her face and her body. Like many Korean immigrant women, she suffered in silence and alone. In the midst of all these difficulties and obstacles, my mother did her best to raise my sister and me. She provided for us in the midst of racism, subordination, sexism, and prejudice. She was a good, kind, compassionate, giving, thoughtful and caring mother. She passed away on January 12, 2010 after fighting a battle with lung cancer.

Now, I can only imagine her sorrow since she did not share with me her own personal stories or her unrealized dreams. Nor did she share her fear, solemnity, and trepidation. Thus I can only imagine the pain, the suffering, and the distress she must have endured during her whole immigrant life. But I do not have to imagine her hard work ethic, diligence, determination, and perseverance that allowed her to survive faithfully in a foreign land. I do not have to imagine her deep love for God, her strong commitment to the church, her constant prayer, and her love for her community and family. On Mother's Day, I do not have to imagine that her Spirit-Chi[18] lives on, as I know it does within my own three children.

What a blessing and privilege it is to be a mother.

Reflection Questions:

1) What is your family's story of immigration?
2) What are you fondest memories of your own parents?
3) How can we instill in our young children today that they are loved no matter what happens?

---

18. Spirit-Chi is the spirit that exists in all of us which gives us energy, warmth and life. For more discussion on Spirit-Chi please see my book, *The Holy Spirit, Chi and the Other* (Palgrave Macmillan, 2011).

28

Women and Men

WHEN I WAS GROWING up, my father would often speak for me. He would introduce me to his friends and then start talking to them on my behalf. He would answer questions that were directed at me and often responded in ways in which I would not have responded. He did this, at least in part, because my ability to speak in Korean was very limited. However he also spoke for my sister and my mother.

I was recently invited to speak on "Business Matters" a television show hosted by Tony Iannelli on Channel 69 in Lehigh Valley, Pennsylvania. I was one of four panelists, joining Kate Wilgruber from the Allentown Women's Center, Dr. Larry Chapp from De Sales University, and Attorney Richard Connell, who were invited to debate the inclusion of coverage for contraceptives in health care packages. The two male panelists opposed the inclusion of contraceptives in health care coverage and the two women panelists supported the inclusion. The debate was lively and sparked good conversation as we spoke from our personal religious beliefs and encounters with women who are in need of good health care.

I frequently disagreed with Dr. Larry Chapp, a Roman Catholic Theologian teaching at De Sales University, a Roman Catholic college. He argued against the morality of using contraceptives and objected to the mandate of providing contraceptives within Roman Catholic institutions and based his argument on the First Amendment. I argued that the current Roman Catholic position on this issue went against Freedom of Religion. A person working in a Roman Catholic hospital, university, or institution is not the same as a member of a church. A worker employed in a Roman Catholic institution does not have to ascribe to the teachings of the church or even need to believe in the Christian God to be employed there. The employee should be given the benefits of any employer working in a non-religious workplace. Thus, it would be against the First Amendment to impose Roman Catholic teachings on the workers and not cover the use of contraceptives for their women employers.

Many Protestants believe that sex is not only for procreation as it is a gift of God. However this understanding is also inherent in the only sanctioned birth control method allowed by Roman Catholic Church: the "rhythm method." With this condoned method there is a recognition that sex does not always lead to procreation. If Roman Catholics truly believe sex is only for procreation why would they even permit the rhythm method?

During the Second Vatican Council (1962–1965) Pope John XXIII asked a commission to examine marriage. The commission consisted of women, laity, priests, and bishops. At the end of the study period the commission endorsed the use of contraceptives. Later, in 1968, Pope Paul VI issued *Humanae Vitae* banned the use of contraceptives and overturned the commission's earlier report. Why wouldn't the commission, which included women and heard the important voices of women on a concern related to women's issues, bodies, health, respect, dignity and well-being, have more validity than men speaking about women without consultation?

As I ponder the argument that the Roman Catholic Church uses today[19], I cannot help but think about how my own father used to speak on my behalf, answer on my behalf, and tell others how I felt. I want to ask today, when will men stop speaking on

---

19. This was written before the accession of Pope Francis in March 2013, and his groundbreaking comments on matters of sexual politics.

behalf of women especially when it pertains directly to women's issues?

I am now a mother of three children and no longer allow my father to speak on my behalf. I believe women of all faith traditions should speak up loud and clear on issues that affect their everyday lives and fight for our human rights.

Reflection Questions:

1) When have you been silenced?
2) How did you find the ability to have your voice heard again?
3) How are women silenced in your community?
4) How do we encourage women to speak?
5) Who are some silenced women that have spoken up and encouraged you?

29

God, Women and the Church

HAWAII!

This land, which surpasses beauty, elegance, harmony, and splendor, is an attractive vacation destination for many people from around the world. Hawaii, a place of warm beaches, palm trees, breathtaking cliffs, and majestic mountains, may seem an unlikely spot for a church meeting. But Hawaii is where twenty-one of us gathered for a "Korean Pastor Theologian Consultation Presbyterian Church (U.S.A.)" from April 9–13, 2012.

The consultation gathered people engaged in different ministries, of different generations, and from different walks of life. We met to discuss, visit, listen to each other's stories, and deepen our own understanding of Koreans and other Asians who traveled to Hawaii to work in the plantations. Through the efforts and hospitality of the Rev. Mary Paik and Dwight Morita, we visited several Asian (or Asian pastored) churches and heard the stories of the struggles, difficulties and joys of building up and maintaining Hawaiian churches. Listening to their stories, many of us realized how their deep history and rich stories have implications for the Korean immigrant churches on the mainland. The consultation also provided time to share our own personal theological reflections

God, Women and the Church

and our struggles of belonging to or pastoring a Korean church in North America today.

Some discussions brought out the multi-layered dilemmas, complexities, and struggles presently experienced by Korean immigrant churches. Issues such as language barriers, intergenerational expectations, gender dynamics, and various forms of ministry engagement came to the forefront.

Among the many topics discussed, it was sexism in all the congregations, as well as internalized sexism in each of us, that really caught my attention. Nine participants were women and all of us, except one, are engaged in ministry outside the Korean American church. There are various reasons for women not to engage in ministry within the Korean American church but the option to work in the Korean American church should be more readily accessible and available. My personal worry is that many female Korean students enter seminary with hopes of serving the Korean American church but never get an opportunity to do so. There appears to be a lack of interest and desire in the Korean American churches to call women pastors. There is also a lack of retention in keeping women as their pastors.

Sexism is present in our churches as well as in our society. However, it may be even more prominent in our Korean American churches due to Korea's cultural history, religious background, and societal values. Churches will give every excuse not to call a woman as their pastor. Churches continue to blame Korean cultural, historical and religious heritages as excuses and reasons for how women are treated in the church. The Rev. Unzu Lee states that "churches have to stop blaming culture" for how the Korean American Churches treat their women. We need to name this systematic subordination and subjugation of women correctly as sexism.

Korean American churches tend to be conservative. The perception of God is that God is masculine and some congregants will publically treat their pastor as a "god." In this manner, we have not come that far from Mary Daly's reality that "if God is male, than male is God." If Korean American churches continue to uphold this paradigm and fail to recognize our own sexism, there will be no room for women's leadership within the church.

Korean American churches cannot continue to blame our history, our Confucian roots, and our cultural practices for the way we perceive and treat women. Korean American churches need to reimagine the way we speak, preach, and teach about who God is. Korean American churches need to embrace the feminine imagery and language about God which is biblically sound and already incorporated into the service books of some dominant mainline churches. We need to reimagine the role of the pastor to allow room for the women's leadership so desperately needed within the Korean American church. If we fail to reinvent our perceptions of women and women's leadership in the church, we will not only have failed our generation but the next generation of Korean Americans.

This fight against sexism within our Korean American churches is an urgent matter. It does not take only one person to work against sexism but the entire church. It does not take only the first generation of Korean immigrants to work against sexism, but the second and third generations as well. It does not only take the leaders to fight against sexism but the entire body of Christ to fight against sexism. This fight against eliminating sexism will move toward healing, embracing, and welcoming Korean American women who are doubly marginalized in our society and the church. It is a difficult battle to fight, but an urgent one that requires the entire body of Christ to work toward the "reign of God" which receives all people as equal regardless of class, age, ethnicity, or gender.

Reflection Questions:

1) How do our churches still reinforce sexism?
2) How can we fight against sexism within our churches?
3) In what ways can we strengthen our churches to become spaces that invite, welcome, include, and value all people regardless of gender, race, social status or sexuality?

4) When have you experienced women's leadership in your church or faith community? When have you experienced women's leadership in society? What have you learned from such experiences?

30

How Can the Church Survive?

MEMBERSHIP IS FALLING IN many mainline denominations. In 2011, the National Council of Churches reported that there was a decline in church membership by about 2% in denominations such as the Lutheran, Episcopal, PC (USA), and Methodist churches. Given this reality, what is the future of the mainline denominational church? How can we survive and be meaningful and relevant to a society where the importance of belonging to a church has been forgotten or dismissed? Will church membership continue to decline because the churches lose the ability to assist those who have been pushed to the margins of society? How can we help our churches grow and survive?

In the spring of 2012, the Rev. Jesse Jackson Sr. visited Lehigh University and Moravian College and participated in two public lectures called, "A Conversation with Rev. Jesse Jackson," moderated by Dr. James Braxton Peterson of Lehigh University and myself.

The conversations were lively, energetic, and prophetic. Each session ended with a 30 minute Q&A period. A Lehigh University student asked the Rev. Jackson, "What is your greatest achievement and why?" The Rev. Jackson had a smile on his face as he swiftly and unexpectedly responded, "Surviving," to which the audience clapped and roared with laughter. After the audience

How Can the Church Survive?

calmed down, he quickly gave a moving, serious, and more elaborate answer to this question by telling a story from his childhood about his father and brother. The fuller answer to the question was very moving, but it was the first impulsive, quick, and unanticipated one that caught me off guard and has stayed with me.

His answer that surviving was his greatest achievement seems astounding when you consider that the Rev. Jackson has worked in and continues to work in many fights for justice and equality. The Rev. Jesse Jackson is well known for his work on civil rights, racial justice, economic equality, and many other issues of our time. He realized early that the economic, racial, gender, sexual, and social structure of society needed to be changed. For the past 50 years, first with the Rev. Dr. Martin Luther King, Jr., and later with his own organization, the Rainbow PUSH Coalition, he has continued this important work.

Perhaps there is some wisdom in the Rev. Jackson's quick answer and surviving is, indeed, one of his great achievements. After all, the impact of the Rev. Jackson's activism has been felt both across the nation and around the world. His fight for freedom and his work with progressive grassroots leaders has endured and been fruitful. And it all stems from his survival.

With all the problems and difficulties of doing ministry in this environment, he has managed to survive all the criticism, racism, and systemic problems that society imposes on those who challenge the status quo. At the Rev. Jackson's 70th birthday celebration held at Georgetown University on November 7, 2011, Dr. Eric Michael Dyson described the Rev. Jackson by quoting Shawn Corey Carter: "there has never been a guy this good for this long." Yes indeed, he has survived.

We have come a long way from the 1950's and the 1960's, but many obstacles still block us from achieving our full humanity and moving forward to the next generation of churches. Some churches and followers of Jesus have always worked for justice. But at the same time, churches have far too often played a major role in maintaining the *status quo* rather than being a prophetic voice to challenge it. Churches blessed slavery when they should have spoken out against it, stayed quiet during the slaughter of 6 million

Jews when it should have worked to stop it. Stood by during the invasion of Iraq[20] when it should have sought peace, and kept women in "their place" when it should have empowered women. Churches have excluded people who are different, marginalized, and not part of the majority or the norm.

All these things leave me with the question: how are we to survive as a church that becomes a beacon of light and hope in this world full of injustices, poverty and inequality? How can we reimagine the role of the church so that we welcome everyone to the table to join in the fellowship and communion of all believers, whether we are rich or poor, men or women, racialized or not, gay or straight? How can the church welcome all people to the table so that the church can be a place where we can encounter God and feel God's love and share God's love in a broken world? How can we survive as a church so that our membership will not decline but grow and flourish?

I also need to ask myself how I can play a role in reshaping the church as a person of color living in a racialized society embedded in racism, sexism, and colonialism. There are lots of battles to be fought and I do hope that I can somehow "survive" them and encourage others to do so.

Reflection Questions:

1) What have you survived in your journey of life?
2) What has your congregation survived over the course of its ministry?
3) How is our church going to survive into the next 50 years?
4) How can we be movers and shakers of the gospel?
5) How can we all be agents of change who help the church to grow?

20. Note that many American churches, including Catholics and Protestants, did object to the Iraqi invasion; however almost all churches that profess a "fundamental" reading of the Bible abstained from objecting to a war whose motives were cloudy at best.

Concluding Thoughts

We live in a world where people from all over the globe come to live as our neighbors. This can cause problems as we try to negotiate different cultures and religious practices and as we seek to raise our children in an ever-globalizing world. However, if we look at this from another perspective, it becomes a wonderful opportunity to live out the gospel. We need to constantly ask ourselves how we "love our neighbor as ourselves" (Mark 12:31).

In a globalizing world, it becomes vitally important to love, welcome, and embrace the stranger and the new immigrants who come to live with us. Rather than building walls around us, we can reflect on how we can reach out to those from whom we differ. We can explore ways to live the gospel with energy, mercy, hope, peace, and love.

This involves living in kindness, peace, and love with others and with ourselves. The inward journey to our inner selves is vitally important. We need to be able to examine our inner selves if we are to love our neighbors as ourselves and live the most fulfilling life possible. This movement towards a better understanding of ourselves will help us understand the One who created us. Understanding the One who created us allows us to reach out in love to our sisters and brothers and all creation.

We need to understand the love that exists within us, and share that love with family and with others. Our journey is an inward journey as well as an outward journey that takes us into the places of the heart.

The journey of life produces joy, happiness, sadness, and love. On that journey, it is important to walk in the path that draws us closer to our Creator and our Sustainer. This journey should move us toward a stronger desire to understand our faith and that we belong to God. As we walk faithfully with God, we will understand that God is ever present in our lives. In the depths, the pain, and the turmoil of our life, God is present. God walks with us and is in tune with us. We are the ones who are often not in tune with God. We need to recognize the fullness of life that can be ours when we walk faithfully with our God whom we experience as the Spirit.

The Spirit God reaches out to us and makes us whole. The Spirit God makes our lives tender as we seek new ways of living in response to God's call. God calls each of us to participate in the movement of the Spirit. This movement can appear to us in many ways. We need to recognize that God will help us in all our efforts to make a change in our world. We need to walk faithfully hand-in-hand with God.

In our faithfulness, we can then recognize that God will help us in all that we do. God will sustain us and keep us even during the difficult times of our lives. Sustained by the Spirit God, we can live a fulfilling life in which we treat others and ourselves as loving creatures of God. This love for each other extends to all of creation and this earth. When it does, we nourish not only each other, but also our planet. The planet is in desperate need of our love and care. By the Spirit's grace, may we respond to that need.

www.ingramcontent.com/pod-product-compliance
Lightning Source LLC
Chambersburg PA
CBHW070921160426
43193CB00011B/1549